SELECTED SPEECHES

O F

FLOYD B. ODLUM

1930 to 1960

SELECTED SPEECHES

OF

FLOYD B. ODLUM

1930 TO 1960

---

*Published by Random House for private distribution
by Floyd B. Odlum*

Manufactured in the United States of America in 1960

Published by Random House, New York, for private distribution by
Floyd B. Odlum, Indio, California

Designed by George Salter

TO

ONE OF OUR GREATEST OF AMERICAN PATRIOTS

MY WIFE

JACQUELINE COCHRAN ODLUM

CONTENTS

~~~~~~~~~~~~~~~~

PREFACE

During the last thirty years my work has taken me into almost every type of business and to many foreign countries. I have watched numerous changes taking place in the political, economic and social fields.

During those years I have had occasion to make many speeches and public statements on diverse subjects. Some of them came again to my attention while I was recently going through old files. A selected few I am having printed and bound together in one volume.

I will give the book principally to school libraries in my home area with the hope that students may benefit from reading it.

A few of my friends will also receive the volume. For each of them some of the speeches or statements will call back memories.

Floyd B. Odlum

November 1960

INTRODUCTION

TO I

A luncheon was held at the Astor Hotel in New York City on June 25, 1930, to honor Rear Admiral Richard E. Byrd on his return from the South Pole.

The speech of welcome was made by me. Mrs. Vincent Astor, on behalf of the American Arbitration Association, presented a medal of appreciation to Rear Admiral Byrd.

I

~~~~~~~~~~~~~~~~~

The American Arbitration Association was, I believe, the last organization to speed Commander Byrd on his way south; and today we have great happiness in being in the vanguard of his host of welcoming friends. The trumpets and drums, streaming ticker tapes, and surging masses of people that greeted him on his arrival in New York six days ago were a fitting tribute to a thrice-returning hero—all the more remarkable because due to radio communication we, in a very real sense, have been living with him constantly since his departure.

The American Arbitration Association, devoted to the peaceful advancement of trade and relations among men, salutes you, Admiral Byrd, who have brought outstanding accomplishment in this field, founded on scientific study and peaceful effort.

Your accomplishments are etched on our memories. We know how in Pensacola you dreamed the dreams that you later made come true. We followed you as Lieutenant in Canada; we thrilled when we heard how you and your not forgotten comrade, Floyd Bennett, winged your way on to the North Pole, with engine spurting oil, disaster imminent; and when a turnabout and return seemed the part of safety, how with broken sextant you returned by dead reckoning in a direct line to your base. The broken sextant and the leaking oil seemed nature's ways of testing you; and you were not found wanting.

And then we watched you, as Commander, bring to a culmination your nonstop flight to France. Those hours in the air, during which you and your comrades carried on, true to your cause, with sight of neither sky above nor of ocean beneath, contributed immeasurably to the progress that aviation has since made. Science and careful planning in advance were here brought to the fine point.

And while the throngs were acclaiming you and the honors were being bestowed, your mind was already occupied with plans for the triumph for which we are again tendering our admiration.

And then during your historic flight to the South Pole we were only seconds behind the residents of Little America in knowing your progress. We were confident of success, because we felt that the forces of nature must give way before organization, planning and daring, all brought into such close focus. Atlas carrying the world on his shoulders was the picture the ancients had of the problem. Our picture today is that of the modern man, pigmy in comparison, leaning over the cockpit of a magical machine which he, himself, has contrived, and watching the world unroll beneath his gaze, while conversing with friends through thousands of miles of space.

The spectacular features stand out as highlights, but not all appreciate in full the background of careful organization, minute planning, and almost uncanny foresight for every contingency. Care, caution, and courage—those three C's of success, were all brought into play in proper balance. While chance could not be eliminated from the stage, she could at least be reduced in role.

A genius for winning and holding men was coupled with high executive ability; and the power to select effective administrators was combined with the spirit that instills into such administrators the determination for enthusiastic effort beyond the full.

In short, in the fields of adventure and exploration have been applied modern business methods in typically an American way. As a result, the home of the blizzard has been studied; more than

150,000 square miles of white spaces on our map have been cleared up by aerial photography; magnetic observations, auroral records, temperature records, and geological studies have enriched science; and radio communication has been advanced.

But beyond the help that has been given to the sciences, beyond the discoveries that have been made, and, most potent of all, is the continuing effect on our youth both of today and of the generations to follow. Because of your success, Admiral Byrd, the pulse of millions beats faster and the determination also to do something big and fine has been rooted deep in countless thousands. Such an influence is deep and illimitable in scope. It quickens the pace of a nation.

Midshipman, Ensign, Lieutenant, Lieutenant Commander, Commander, Rear Admiral—these are the measures of progress. Scrolls, keys, medals and citations—these are fitting tributes, the modern laurels. But when the laurel loses its freshness, and the din in the streets dies away, the accomplishments will remain, and the dynamic personality of Admiral Byrd will carry on and on in its influence on others.

And so it is to the individual, to our fellow being, Dick Byrd, whose dynamic personality, whose courage, whose determination have kept the fires of ambition burning brightly that I today bear the imperishable intangibles: hope, honor, and affection.

We are glad you are home, Admiral. We know that some new venture will soon be claiming you, because men such as you must keep going on and on. This thought was remarkably well expressed by our poet Edwin Markham, when he penned the following lines to Admiral Byrd:

> The men of dauntless heart have willed and won;
>> The impossible is done!
> And now they call us from the upper air
>> To leave the old and take the lyric dare—
> To hazard the incredible advance,
>> To seize dominion over circumstance!

For the rise of man is endless;
  Every goal is only a tavern for his marching soul,
Only a camp for the night
  In man's eternal flight.

Yes, sometime he will pass the earthly bars,
  Laugh and reach out his hand among the Stars.

INTRODUCTION

TO II

For several years I served as head of the American Arbitration Association. Herewith is one of the many speeches I made to further the cause of arbitration.

It was delivered on May 29, 1931, before the National Foreign Trade Council and the subject was "Arbitration as an Aid to Foreign Trade."

II

~~~~~~~~~~~~~~~~~~

With respect to the subject matter of my talk today, I have two particular interests: (1) as one interested in arbitration as such and as an officer of the American Arbitration Association; and (2) as one actively engaged in investments and work abroad. The corporations with which I am associated develop and operate public utilities. In recent years we have extended our efforts to foreign countries and today we operate in thirteen foreign countries. It seems, at first blush, a far cry from the public utility business, which is essentially one dealing with immovable plants, to the export business, which is one dealing in movement in commodities. But there is a very real connection. The day has passed when any one believes that one country can prosper permanently at the expense of others. A prosperous nation is a good customer for trade. "Trade" means barter and exchange. When we sell something we must get something in return. Money is not that something. It is only a medium, a method of keeping a running account, so to speak, a token of something tangible to follow. That something can be goods brought into this country, or it can be property acquired abroad and left abroad. I conceive that my company, having permanently invested, in recent years, more than $500,000,000 in property abroad, has not only improved the buying power of these peoples, but it has, to the amount of its expenditures, reduced the amount of credits or per contra the purchase of foreign goods that would have been necessary to enable us to carry on the export trade which we actually did carry on. I go so far as to affirm that we did not send those $500,000,000 abroad but that, indirectly, we really sent goods abroad. I, therefore, feel a part and parcel of, and vitally interested in, our export trade.

It has been both my duty and privilege to spend most of the last five years abroad traveling about in Latin America and Europe making such investments. During the forepart of this period I watched from the other side, so to speak, our foreign trade and our foreign credits grow hand in hand and, with them, our prosperity at home and our influence abroad. And then I watched the decline of our loans and foreign trade, aggravated, it is true, by other factors, but still with money and goods the principal actors on the stage. I saw what seemed to be almost paradoxes. I wondered why so many of the people should be on a black bread diet while we and others had all that wheat. I wondered why we, with all that surplus gold and surplus food and surplus goods, should feel so poor—why we should suddenly become the world's "poor little rich boy." Sitting in Rumania, I wondered why that country, so rich in natural resources and barren of local industries, should be so sadly in need of farm equipment and other industrial products while we had them in surplus, and why interest rates there were, in practice, as high as 15 to 20 percent, while dollars were actually on the financial bread line in New York. I concluded, from this wondering, that something that was essentially dynamic had become static.

I have just returned from six months in Europe and I return an optimist. I disagree with those who believe that American business is adrift or that the capitalistic system has failed. That balance wheel in the equilibrium of our whole structure, our exportable surplus, will be satisfactorily adjusted by those represented here today. I feel, while facing you, that I am looking squarely into the eyes of returning prosperity. The difficulties experienced have momentarily turned our leadership in another direction, namely, a rigid examination by businessmen of their enterprises, to find where mistakes have been made, where waste has occurred and where expansion, or particularly further expansion, would be ill judged. We have been too busy progressing to give these factors adequate attention.

As Clark Minor, of the International General Electric Company, recently stated: "Foreign commerce has become a plant requiring careful attention and a highly specialized cultivation if it is to thrive at all." It has been my observation that, in such cultivation, we have neglected certain intangibles which may readily turn the scale in our favor in many cases of competition. One of these intangibles of great potentiality is commercial arbitration. Good will of our buyers is of greatest importance. A difference between buyer and seller quickly, inexpensively and amicably settled usually retains the customer, while a dispute usually loses the customer. I do not refer to hasty attempts at good will proceedings when ill will has already gained the upper hand, but, rather, to our willingness to provide in our contracts a method of settlement which will work automatically to preserve good will when a question arises.

There is the greatest difference between the use of arbitration in our domestic and our foreign trade. In domestic trade the development of arbitration has been truly remarkable. The members of approximately 500 trade organizations here use arbitration as a method of settling controversies. They do this by including arbitration clauses in their contracts. Arbitration outside trade bodies shows a similar tendency. The American Arbitration Tribunal, following a demand, is now organized to operate in approximately 1,800 of our cities on the request of either party to a contract. A standard practice has been adopted and scores of trade organizations are affiliated with the movement to maintain a national system of arbitration based on this practice. The courts show an eagerness to uphold arbitration and lawyers are taking up the practice, seeing, not a menace, but an opportunity to serve their clients. Arbitration, as standard practice, has lifted from American domestic trade an immense load of expense and worry.

Arbitration in foreign trade presents a sharp contrast. In the importing groups there has been a decided awakening to the importance of arbitration. But this is based on the belief that arbitration will take place in the United States under our standard rules of practice. It is when we examine the export field that the unsolved difficulty arises. Arbitration, fully to meet the requirements, should (1) be at small cost; (2) be expeditious; (3) be a determination on facts and evidence and not a compromise; (4) be final and not end in litigation; (5) have the support of the courts so that the award is final with force of judgment and so that no suit can be brought while arbitration is pending. These requirements have been met in the United States. A large number of leading citizens—1,000 in New York alone—have agreed to serve the American Arbitration Association as arbitrators without pay. The courts have upheld the award in the exceedingly few cases (less than one-half of one percent) that have been subject to court attacks. From the standpoint of foreign trade we are in admirable shape with respect to courts. Under the United States Arbitration Law and under the laws of the port states, both on the Atlantic and Pacific seaboards, an arbitration agreement, either for an existing or a future dispute, is legally enforceable; the courts will stay an action at law until the arbitration has been held and will direct the arbitration to proceed when a party obstructs it. Also, an award rendered is enforceable as a judgment of court.

In pointing out how arbitration can be of aid to foreign trade, we have two questions to answer:

Has the American businessman adequate security in an arbitration held outside the United States and, if not, can he get it?

Whether true or not, the average businessman thinks the answer to the first question is "No" and, as a consequence, he does not resort to arbitration. Those of you who attended the International Chamber of Commerce meeting in Washington must have been struck by the statement that, over a period of eight years, but one case involving an American was settled by arbitration in the arbitral court of the Chamber and that, whenever requested to arbitrate, the American refused unless he had subscribed to a compulsory clause; and in only two instances, so far as available data showed, had the foreign merchants been successful in getting the American to use the Chamber of Commerce Clause. This spells a feeling of insecurity.

Can conditions be changed so as to increase the feeling of security?

I think they can: first, by bringing together a group of men interested in foreign trade to work out a program similar to that developed in this country, and then by inviting and urging its acceptance upon those with whom we do business in foreign countries. American trade agencies abroad might well cooperate. I am happy to say that the American Manufacturers Export Association, the National Council of American Importers and Traders and many other organizations are cooperating with the American Arbitration Association in obtaining the necessary information to consider such a plan, and I hope the National Council on Foreign Trade will join with this group. The American Manufacturers Export Association has recently sent out a questionnaire to all its members and, from replies received, is enthusiastic about the results that might be accomplished.

I believe arbitration a distinct aid to foreign trade in holding the business after it has been originally procured. My conclusion, based on watching the operations of our competitors abroad, is that we do not always, or as much as we should, harmonize with the psychology and what might be considered the peculiarities of the people with whom we are conducting business. Many times I have seen business go to other quarters because the representative of our competitor becomes a native in manners and customs and methods of approach, while we stand too much on the merits of our products and on our rights. In the case of our own companies, we become in fact a part of the community served. Their problems are ours also and their success ours.

The theory of arbitration is well developed abroad where the individuals are accustomed to international transactions in their daily life, and in transactions in which neither party has a desire to submit to the jurisdiction of the other party's court. But the mechanics of arbitration are most poorly devised, with no uniformity. Europe is ideal for an all-embracing arbitral body having a panel of reputable professional and businessmen from the various countries to draw upon.

It is the practice of our companies uniformly to insert an arbitration clause in our agreements, even in our franchise contracts with public authorities. And they have worked well. They carry with them the rather convincing belief that we are willing to give and take as justice requires and as that justice is promptly determined by an ordinary man or group of men of understanding, rather than to depend on technical legal rights. The conveyance of such a belief carries with it good will. Within the last sixty days I had an arbitration case with a European firm in which more than $400,000 was at issue. The arbiter was furnished written briefs and, one week later, an afternoon was devoted by the parties to oral discussion of the problem with the arbiter. The following morning the award was made. That it was in our favor was satisfying, but that when, a few days later, I met the people who were on the other side of the case, they did not even refer to the award, but as sincere friends who had an honest difference of opinion which had been settled and forgotten, proceeded to further business associations, was even more important and much more gratifying. And that is rather typical of most arbitration cases. They often serve as the foundation for firmer friendships rather than enmities. Not long ago two parties submitted a controversy of long standing to the American Arbitration Association. They were given the Tribunal Chambers and asked to agree on a written submission of the issues. When the clerk went in later to get the submission he found them drafting a contract for a further piece of business. Once they had agreed to accept the views of a competent third party, their own differences became of minor importance and their future business relations of great importance.

News dealing with firms, individuals and methods travels fast in foreign lands—much faster, I believe, than here where we have no borders. When we have a pleasant or an unpleasant experience over some difference with a customer, it gets into circulation and nationals of one country often follow the friendly influence of others that do business with us. Arbitration can generally be counted on to build up our reputation and to help with new customers in strange places.

In the strenuous days of competition in foreign trade, time will be of importance, and arbitration is a time-saver. For example, under our Tariff Act, customs duties can be refunded if goods are returned for nonconformity to specifications within thirty days after release from customs. An attempted return usually initiates a controversy. Arbitration is the only judicial proceeding that can dispose of such controversy within the thirty-day period. Also, the privacy of arbitration has a real bearing. A law suit, with attendant publicity of evidence, often does more harm to the successful litigant than the judgment does good. It is a case of a successful operation, followed by the death of the patient.

Good will, good relations and good reputation are among the most valuable of business assets. I have talked with many foreigners on the subject of arbitration, and I am convinced it is one of the important ways to foster good will, good relations and good reputation. Foresight should lead us in the direction of an American plan which will do for foreign trade what arbitration is so surely accomplishing in domestic trade.

INTRODUCTION

TO III

The following speech on the subject of "Investment Trusts" was made by me on May 7, 1934, before the Harvard School of Business Administration.

At the time, Atlas Corporation was transforming itself into an investment company, more like the English "finance company" than the English "investment trust."

My checks had shown that the oldest and one of the most respected English investment trusts, over the first fifty years of its life prior to 1934, had averaged an annual return of about 5¾% on its capital. The English finance companies, taking greater risks, were expected to do somewhat better.

Atlas Corporation has in fact done much better. During the thirty-year period prior to my retirement in 1960 as chief executive, the dividends paid plus the increase of asset value of the common stock amounted to more than 800% of the asset value of the common stock at the beginning of such period, which averages out to considerably better than 25% per year on the asset value of the common stock at the beginning of the period.

No single year within the period conformed to such average because there are cycles in the "special situation" business with consequent intermediate ups and downs. These cycles have little to do with the concurrent trends in the general stock market. The company has been experiencing the downbeat of such a cycle recently. Otherwise the average result as stated above would have been considerably better.

The average result from the start of the company (through direct predecessors) in 1923 would be even better than stated for the thirty-year period. Even if the high point of the stock market in 1929 had been taken as the starting point, the average result would have been better than 15% per year. It has been my belief that an average result of better than 6% per year justifies the business of the company for the reasons stated in the accompanying speech. My objective during my direction of the affairs of the company was a result approaching 10% per year on capital employed.

III

〜〜〜〜〜〜〜〜〜〜

I will in a brief way attempt to discuss the history of the investment trust, the vicissitudes through which it has passed at home and abroad, its present status, and finally the part which it may be expected to play in the future and the type of service which the American public may be expected to demand. This covers a fairly wide field and consequently only general statements and fundamental facts can be indulged in.

First we shall consider the British and Scottish investment trusts.

It was in a period of superabundance of capital needing employment, back about the time of our Civil War, that the idea of the investment trust germinated. In the beginning there was no thought of just creating something which the public could be induced to buy. The first investment trusts were not begotten by promoters but to fill a pressing need. Perhaps this is one of the reasons why the principle has so steadily held its own.

The need for the good offices of the investment trust in the times which brought it into being is outlined as follows by the *London Economist* of April 12, 1862. This was a period when the mills of Manchester were shut down for lack of cotton and England's surplus capital was unemployed. I quote as follows:

"Many of the schemes which now try to attract the public are good, but some of them, by the mere doctrine of chances, must also be bad. Nor can any certain rule be laid down for the general guidance of the whole public. Business would be infinitely easier than it now is if a few precepts or a doctrinaire theory would tell us how to succeed in it. But one rule may be laid down which is very simple and, if acted on, would be very efficacious. People should only engage in what they understand. Money is a serious thing and we should only invest it in undertakings we comprehend and venture it in risks we appreciate. . . . There is no royal road to the knowledge of money matters, and those who fancy that there is will expiate their vanity by a diminution of their income. If country clergymen, if maiden ladies will engage in undertakings which it requires a practiced mind to estimate and much effort even of that practiced mind to comprehend and master, they must not complain of the fate which they may expect and which in some sense they deserve. Involuntary victims justly claim our pity, but voluntary victims must not hope for it."

In England and Scotland the investment trust was a partial answer to the question of helping the investor find a way to employ funds.

The very first trusts that operated in Great Britain were unincorporated private associations. Their managers acted as trustees, and participation in these joint ventures passed from hand to hand by the sale of certificates. England was sending much of her unemployed capital abroad. There was great need for careful study of world conditions. The data were very sketchy, the need for trained analysts and students of government finance was obvious. It was also obvious that the field was not one in which the individual could be expected to exercise judgment, good or bad, being quite without any adequate information. The people known as investment trust managers took on this task and the capital that was placed in their hands was the investment trust.

The unincorporated association was declared illegal, but the decision was later reversed. Anyway, they had grown beyond their first crude form of organization and were being incorporated. The Lord Justice in this decision said they [the certificate holders] acted under what "was nothing but a trust deed for the purpose of securing a good investment spread over a number of securities so that one might equalize another." The name of investment trust given to these first cooperative groups clung when it was no longer truly descriptive, crossed the water, and remains with us today. The reasons given by the judge are still good.

The first general advertisement of an incorporated investment trust that I find appeared in the pages of the *Economist* in March 1883. It was that of the Foreign, American and General Investment Trust Company, Limited, which is still in existence.

Many others were organized until the combined capital of the English investment trusts, speaking in very approximate terms, is today about $1,500,000,000. It has always been the policy of the English trust managers to keep each trust comparatively small. Usually, instead of issuing more shares after the trust has reached a certain size, a new one is organized. One organization will manage a whole group of these trusts. Some are formed with limited powers as to types of investment, for example, securities of one industry only, or foreign securities only, but usually this is not the case.

The usual structural pattern of these trusts has been debentures, preferred stock and common stock, arranged at the beginning, generally with about one third of the capital represented by each class of security.

The investment trust in England and Scotland looked in those days and still does to income from interest and dividends primarily and to increase of basic capital values only secondarily. This was considered conservative practice and their securities were held by conservative investors. The debenture, being well secured, sold on a low yield basis and the same was true of the preferred stock to a lesser degree. Now if $300 is raised, one third on debentures paying 4 percent interest, one third on 5 percent preferred and one third on common stock, and if a 6 percent net return after expenses is obtained on the securities in which the money is invested, it follows that $18 will be earned, of which $4.00 will be paid as debenture interest, $5.00 as preferred stock dividend, leaving $9.00 for the common stock or 9 percent on the money invested in the common stock. An 8 or 9 percent return was considered handsome to compensate for risking money to the extent it was risked in the common stock. This combination of a 6 percent return with some small opportunity for capital appreciation, with that 6 percent return spread over a three-layer capital structure of bonds, preferred stock and common stock, is pretty much the story of the functioning of the average English investment trust.

We should, in order to cover the ground which I have mapped out for this brief survey, turn back here for a moment. There was another development which took place along with that which has just been described.

British capital was very alert in seeking employment, but even giving the big majority of Englishmen and Scotsmen full credit for caution and conservatism, the times called for the venturesome spirit and many had it beyond the 8 or 9 percent category. Railways were building, cities were building, the world was expanding in area and at the same time being brought closer together in improved transportation and communication, and England was the world's banker in every sense.

In no small part, the participation of English capital in this field of greater risk and greater possibilities of profit took the form of the so-called finance company (as distinct from the investment trust), an organization quite new in those days to Throgmorton Street; and, being new and essentially more speculative, it was the cause of much comment and criticism. Turning again to the pages of the *Economist* (July 1864) we find detailed discussion.

"The financial world is full of rumors as to the great profits recently earned by the new finance companies and the great dividends they are about to pay."

A month later: "We hear just now in some quarters so much censure of finance companies that it is proper we should distinctly see what is the true function of such companies and what is not; what is the use of them, and what their abuse; what is the exact evil for which we censure them and what the precise good we should expect from them. It is perfectly certain that the existence of such companies is *fixed*. . . .

"There are several modes in which a finance company can legitimately and profitably employ a large capital; profitably we mean in both its meanings—in the sense of getting a good dividend for themselves, and of doing much good to the public at large. First, they may lend on what we may call good but *curious* securities. There are many securities in the market which are a little out of the common way, but very good. They need investigation but they bear it. . . .

"Secondly. Nothing can be more within the rules of legitimate business than buying shares or other property when unduly depressed and selling it when the public has come to understand it, and its price has therefore risen. . . .

"Thirdly. These finance companies may introduce other companies. . . . The public naturally wants a guide for its investments, when so many and such various proposals are made to it; and the natural guides are finance companies of large capital, high position and proved judgment. . . . It is commonly objected that finance companies themselves take shares in these dependent companies and are, therefore, not to be attended to. But if they did *not* take shares *we* at least should not attend to them. If they were not prepared to risk their own money, we should not much regard their advice to obtain people to risk theirs."

So here we have the English so-called finance company, which has grown up alongside the English investment trust.

The differences between these two classes of companies are principally as follows:

1. The investment trust looks more to regular dividend and interest income, while the finance company looks more to profits through underwritings, rising value of their securities and subsequent sale.
2. The investment trust only pays out as interest and dividends what it receives as regular interest and dividend income. Profits on sales of securities are not carried to the income account but are carried to reserves and used to write down cost of securities owned in the portfolio, or to offset depreciation in market value of securities if there has been such depreciation. The investment trust does not have to pay an income or profits tax on such capital profits. The finance company carries its profits on underwritings and promotions and stock sales to its profit account, can pay them out as dividends and pays a tax on them.
3. The income of the investment trust is more stable, but the opportunity for profits is greater in the finance company.

It is sufficient to say that our income tax law treating market profits as income effectually prevents the adoption here of the practice of the English investment trust as to reserves.

It remains to be said also that however much one may admire the stout conservative spirit which has built up the British and Scottish investment trusts, it is to be doubted whether the American investor could be brought to place the same emphasis upon straight income return and be content to watch the slower augmentation of his principal.

Managers of investment funds in this country must not only take this attitude of their shareholders into account but they must also consider whether or not a fuller opportunity may not lie in taking at least a part of a leaf from the book of the finance companies.

There is another distinction between the trust company and the finance company which should be mentioned. The investment trusts have paid dividends when it might be said upon strict analysis that their capital was impaired. As an example taken at random from the list, one of the leading trusts showed (January 1, 1934) assets at market values of £1,757,500 against liabilities of £2,305,000. Yet the company paid a dividend of 5 percent upon its ordinary shares. The finance companies may not be so trustful of the future. They may make distribution only when their capital remains intact after such payment.

To sum up the English situation: The accumulated capital in Great Britain was obliged to seek opportunity abroad, a process altogether too expensive for the individual. The development of new countries required special study and acquaintance. The three-ply combination of debentures, preference shares and common shares permitted all classes of investors to participate in various proportions as to risk. The results reflected credit upon the managers. As their prestige grew they were invited to sit in conferences concerning new issues. It came to be said of new flotations, if the investment trusts buy the public will buy. That they clung to their investment business and rigidly kept their underwriting profits in place as a by-product is perhaps in part the reason they have retained their following. The investment trust is a permanent and important part of financial England. Together with the more speculative finance companies they represent a powerful influence on English financial policies and investments abroad. During the panic of 1893 and subsequent years, losses occurred in income and assets, and reorganizations occurred. Subsequent years enabled management to record values and income.

Now I shall speak of American trusts.

The history of investment trusts in this country is a fantastic chapter. As late as 1925 they were generally unknown. In 1926 and 1927, the idea was introduced and began to interest the public. It was a matter of education and it is a tribute to the soundness of the principle that the public liked it so well that it overlooked the necessity of management trained in hard-boiled analysis and immune to the lure of market profits.

In 1929, as the market reached its apex, there were some 640 trusts, big and little, enumerated, with net assets estimated at $4,000,000,000. The year was a mad one for the promoter up to the time of the crash in October. Of the new financing in that year of $6,250,000,000, investment companies accounted for a full third. It has been estimated that the public subscribed $1,000,000,000 for various trust offerings in August and September alone.

During this period the offerings made to the public were sponsored for the most part by investment banking houses, both large and small. It was a misfortune for all concerned that our investment houses were quite new to the idea of management and continuing responsibility. The public became possessed of the idea that huge market profits could be garnered by this new instrumentality without risk. The misfortune may be said to have fallen alike upon promoter and shareholder. The so-called managements paid the penalty of ignorance. It is known that in more than one case, huge amounts of cash rolled in to hands that were quite without any kind of a program as to its disposition. Whereas British trusts sold and still sell on the basis of asset value plus management, some of our companies in 1930 and subsequent years sold below asset value, drastically discounting management.

The term "investment trust" has never had exactly the same meaning here that it has in England. It originally covered here a multitude of different kinds of companies which could more properly have been described as incorporated pools of capital. Some of them were blind pools. Some went in for particular classes of securities like aviation, railroad or public utility. All or substantially all were for the purpose of making stock market profits and not for the obtaining of fixed income. Some had limitations in their charter as to the percentage of capital that could be invested in any one company, country or class of security. Some had four or five classes of securities, some three, some two and some one. There was no rule about anything. Most of them were made to sell. The promoter was thinking more of the commission on the original sale, the management fee and bonus stock and the subsequent brokerage on portfolio transactions, than of ultimate results or long-range investment policies. Then came the crash—investment trust stocks that had mounted market-wise to way above their asset value or capitalized earning power began falling. They were not in investors' hands. For the most part they were so-called green goods. They did not stop falling when they reached asset value. They kept on going down until the management which had been at a 100 percent premium was at a discount, sometimes a very heavy one as measured by difference between asset values and market values. This presented an opportunity to those willing or able to see it and take advantage of it to buy securities below their current market values by buying indirectly into the portfolios of investment trusts through purchase of such trusts' outstanding stocks. By buying control one could take over management and readjust the portfolio to suit one's ideas or to stop falling values by conversion into cash. This is how Atlas Corporation built a trust up from $15,000,000 to $125,000,000 during the depression, and how we increased the asset value of its common stock approximately 100 percent during a period of falling prices—we took control of some twenty-two trusts in total. Many of them have since been absorbed completely by the parent company.

The complete loss of confidence in management caused some concerns interested in selling securities to develop a new type of trust, called the fixed trust. In essence, a particular lot of securities was purchased and allotments in this aggregate were sold to small investors. The cost of selling was about 10 to 12 percent so the investor was paying about this premium to have someone select a list of securities for him to purchase. But the trust was usually arranged so that the portfolio securities, once purchased, could not be sold except on the happening of certain contingencies and then must be sold. No management was provided. Management was abhorrent to the taste. A security even though falling in price because of decreased earnings and probability of dividend cessation could not be sold. When the dividend ceased and consequently the market in the stock hit bottom, it had to be sold. Under this sort of setup, of course, losses were inevitable and the fixed trust passed into oblivion. In its place sprang up a semi-fixed trust that had some management features. More management features were added from time to time as new semi-fixed trusts were formed, until many of the newer ones are really orthodox trusts with management.

Then there was the so-called open end trust—like one or more kinds of the other trusts except that the stockholder could turn in his shares at any time and get their current asset value less some arbitrary amount or percent, and new shares were always being sold to keep up the size of the trust.

Many of the fixed trusts are still in existence with no way to eliminate them from the scene. They are known as orphans in many cases because their sponsors have also disappeared from the scene. The fixed trust was not altogether a post-crash development. Several date back to as early as 1924. Many, when there was real sponsorship, have been traded into a present-day form of semi-management trust under the same sponsorship.

The investment trusts in this country are still in their formative stage, but the picture is taking shape. Out of the mass there remain about a dozen leading trusts of the management type and a few smaller ones. None of them function along the strictly English lines. They partake more of the nature of the English finance company. This is natural because the people of this new country are still thinking more of profits than of income. Here we generally measure a man's wealth by his assets. In England his wealth is generally measured by his annual income. The common stockholder here, speaking in general terms, is interested more in the asset value, and increase of asset value, than he is in the earning power.

The managements that have lasted through the depression have become solidified, organized and skilled in selection and appraisal of securities.

In this country the average investor of moderate means has not the facilities or the ability to make good investment of his money. The investment trust can fill a great need by acting in effect as the manager for groups of these small investors called stockholders. The investment trust organization is at the center of things, knows finance, trends of business and politics, and has access to up-to-the-minute data about various companies and securities. The organization can do all the work for a small percentage of the assets administered, which is cheap when analyzed from the standpoint of each individual stockholder investor. Also in union there is strength. These stockholder investors, by pooling their funds together, are able to get bargains that they would not get individually. The pool of capital can buy blocks of good stocks in distress because of bank loans against them or for other reasons. Also they can direct or participate in reorganizations and possibly even underwritings of securities with resultant profits.

The new Securities Act curtails the past functions of the investment banker. It is probable that the investment trust will have a large place in future big-scale financing here, as the English investment trusts have in England. The trusts will work more and more together on matters of policy.

Some, in the course of time, will lean toward the policy of the standard English trust. Others—the majority—will, in keeping with the general run of American ideas and demands, be more like the English finance company. More and more they work toward a two- or three-ply structure, that is either preferred stock and common stock, or bonds, preferred stock and common stock. Thus, each class will get income or security commensurate with the risk taken by that class.

The confidence in investment trusts is reviving. Their shares are no longer at discount. Management is again at par. The leverage that a preferred stock gives to a financial structure with rising price levels is recognized, and common stocks with such leverage quality are for the most part at a premium over asset values. The need for a properly run investment trust is real. Their place in the scheme of things is a big one. I think you will hear more about them as time goes on.

In closing let me say we have heard much commendation for English trust results of management and much criticism of American management and results. One cannot organize companies in times of high price levels with an eye to profit rather than income and expect favorable results at the end of a subsequent depression. One can organize a company for the securing of a safe, conservative income and succeed quite well over a term of years, notwithstanding intervening depressions. But too many embarrassing questions must not be asked about asset values of stock companies during periods of low price levels. Some of us might believe that if a company gains 6 percent in income on its cost of portfolio and loses 20 percent in principal values during any year, there has been a net loss to the stockholder; and viewed this way the English trusts do not stand out in such rosy colors. I recently took at random about a dozen of the old English investment trusts and about a dozen formed from 1925 to 1929. When their portfolios were taken at market values and not cost, only four of the old companies and none of the younger ones could show unimpaired capital. Many had lost the entire common stock capital and some a major part of the preferred stock capital.

Then I took occasion to check the history of what I believe to be the oldest incorporated English investment trust. Its senior securities have paid regularly 5 percent since 1880. Its common stock started at 6 percent, rose gradually to 8 in 1889, fell away to 6, 5½ and 5 and then 4½ during the depression years of 1892 to 1897, then built up slowly to 8 percent in 1914 with pretty fair stability around 7 percent until the recent depression, when the rate had gotten down to 5 percent again. The company had about an 8 percent impairment of capital at the beginning of this year. The fact therefore is that the managers, over the life of the company, have earned about 5¾ percent on the funds paid in to them and placed under their control.

Now this result is good or bad according to your viewpoint. The average American would consider it not so good, believing that skilled management should average more than 6 percent when not limited to high-grade low-yield investments. The average Englishman would probably consider it good, particularly when the balance is struck at the conclusion of a depression.

INTRODUCTION

TO IV

In 1937, after long investigation by the Securities and Exchange Commission, regulation of Investment Trusts was about to be proposed to Congress.

My recommendations as shown on the following pages were submitted to the Commission on July 2, 1937. I have omitted portions of what I said to avoid as much as practicable duplication of statements in the speech before the Harvard School of Business Administration.

IV

~~~~~~~~~~~~~~~~~~~~

R estriction and regulation of private business by the Government is justified when necessary in the public interest. But it should not be introduced except when public interest requires it, and even then, should leave private business as free as public interest permits. The study, of which this statement is a part, covers a widely divergent group of companies, loosely and, as to most at least, wrongly classified together as "Investment Trusts and Companies." No general restriction or regulation could properly apply equally to them all. As to their policies of operation and investment, it is something that concerns primarily the company and its own stockholders. The laws under which the Securities and Exchange Commission operates in large measure at least already cover the issue and sale of their securities. There is a field for permissive restriction and regulation to which the term "Investment Trust" could logically be applied. These points will be touched on in greater detail.

In the United States the terms "Investment Trust" and "Investment Company" have no fixed meaning. The companies that are popularly referred to under this classification vary widely as to the purposes for which organized, charter powers, types of investors that hold their stocks and fields of actual operations. There is no more sound reason to measure them all by the same yardstick or to apply to them the same rules, restrictions and limitations than there is, for example, to require automobile companies, chain stores and oil companies all to operate in the same way.

The powers, duties and responsibilities of directors and officers and the rights of stockholders are about the same, or should be, in the case of all kinds of companies, whether the capital is in steel, oil, automobiles or securities. Therefore, *special* legislation or regulation in respect of such powers, duties and responsibilities for "Investment Trusts" seems illogical, for if it should be required for one group it must be needed for the others. There may be a difference, let us say, in facilities for management due to the fact that one type deals in liquid capital while the other does not. If so, then the special legislation or regulation should be directed to the problems raised by such difference.

There are in the aggregate a large group of people (such, for example, as those who have been left with small or medium-sized estates) who desire or need a little more income than can be had from interest on savings deposits or from public bonds or from the usual type of trust funds which are limited to high-grade low-yield bonds legal for savings bank investments. These people can ill afford to take much risk of loss or diminished return. Here is a field not now adequately served where useful work can be done by trained conservative investment experts. Let such a field be served by a type of company to be defined as an "Investment Trust" so restricted, regulated or safeguarded that conservatism and continuity of income will be the keynote. Require it, if you please, to have only one class of outstanding stock and no debt, and to have its investments well diversified as to companies, industries, classes of securities and marketability; but not so restricted as are savings banks or trust funds. The people who want that kind of investment will know what they can logically expect. And a lot of people will invest in such a company and properly so.

But there are a lot of other investors who are working or otherwise productively engaged and building up a surplus of earnings who have neither the training nor the facilities to search out investments or to know them when found (such, for example, as the doctor, the lawyer, and numerous other classes busy with their own affairs), who desire a somewhat greater rate of return than provided by savings banks or the highest grade bonds, and also want some opportunity for appreciation of capital. For this they are willing to assume a degree of risk not proper for the type of "Investment Trust" investor mentioned above. Now, certainly, a company serving in the main this type of investor should not operate in the restricted regulated way I have defined above for a type to be called "Investment Trusts." Make it illegal for any other type to call itself an "Investment Trust," but don't make all companies conform to the same pattern simply because they invest in securities.

There is a field of finance never yet adequately served in America and which, I believe, can only be well served by large companies and with benefit both to industry as a whole and to the stockholders. I refer to the many industrial and other companies that have a sound place in the scheme of things, but have fallen on evil days because of lack of working capital, dry rot in the management or inability to carry through some temporary period. Sometimes their capital structure must be adjusted, sometimes new blood must be injected into the administrative department. Their affairs are in such shape that a short-term bank loan will not suffice or would not be justified from the bankers' standpoint. These securities, although sound, are unseasoned and should not be distributed to the general public until "proven." It is no place for the stock broker's services and the investment banker must promptly resell what he buys. Much unnecessary loss has been caused untold investors in such companies because in this country there have been no organized groups of capital for such situations. Such capital must be semi-mobile and must be backed by guiding hands ready to temporarily take hold, diagnose and help solve corporate situations. This is a field in which the investment trusts in England engage to considerable degree, and also the English so-called finance companies. It is a field in which Atlas Corporation, which I head, has interested itself. No legislation or regulation should be adopted that would cut off development of service in this field or cause companies so operating to be bound by like rules of capitalization, investment, operation or relation to other companies as apply to companies referred to above as "Investment Trusts."

Mistakes of judgment are inherent in human nature, even among experts and in high places. Isolated cases of breach of trust and thievery will occur. We already have sufficient laws to cover this. The typical or recurrent type of so-called abuses that affect the public interest and welfare and cannot be prevented by present legislation are the ones that would call for preventive regulation. I consider the present laws under which the Securities and Exchange Commission operates both broad and beneficial. I have not had the benefit of the results of the study which your Commission has made, but if you have uncovered types of recurrent abuses in the so-called investment trust field, I would be disappointed to find that they were not largely eliminated or could be through exercise of your Commission's present powers. I doubt if many of them could happen if complete full disclosures of the transactions had been mandatory. If not prevented by the mere certainty of disclosure, stockholders advised of the transaction would usually have adequate remedy. Therefore, I urge you first, if practicable, to measure your present powers to cure continuing abuses before drafting *new* legislation to cure previous abuses of types no longer existing.

Of course, I realize that it may be necessary and proper for a public representative to have some degree of effective powers to check and to see that there has been or will be adequate presentation of facts.

Personally, I would welcome some public body or arbiter who could pass on the equities as between divergent interests in such matters as mergers, reorganizations and exchanges of securities, not to substitute his judgment for that of the management, but to see that things are at least within the range of upper and lower limits within which reasonable men can properly differ.

Every company today that wishes either to sell its securities to the public or list its securities on a stock exchange must file with the Securities and Exchange Commission such detailed information as to deter or prevent transactions harmful to the interests of the companies or their stockholders. The Commission has very broad powers as to information, rules and regulations.

Security holders equipped with such full information should be in position to exact recourse under the many existing laws from a management with sufficient temerity to engage in improper transactions in the face of almost certain discovery. Already corporate executives walk through a maze of laws and regulations too complicated and numerous to follow. There are hundreds of ways to catch the wrongdoer, all open incidentally to the idle lawyer who has no business of a more constructive nature than to attempt to snare the man of honest practice and good intentions. The purpose of legislation is not to harass business. If in the public interest there seems need for law or regulation in the field of this study, by all means let us have it, but not in such form that it deals or leaves supervising bureaus to deal with matters that should be left to management or to decisions by stockholders, or in such form that would be likely to substitute the judgment of a public authority without personal responsibility to shareholders for the judgment of executives and directors who have such direct responsibility, or, what is equally bad, keep good men out of the field who would not care to have their judgment warped or their characters and careers jeopardized by an outside body whose very questioning with attendant publicity has oftentimes the practical effect of indictment and conviction.

Companies, other than those I have referred to as conservative and diversified "Investment Trusts," should have wide managerial latitude in the amount of capital invested in any company, in-

dustry or situation. Times change, natural requirements and desires of stockholders change. The right of stockholders to run
their own affairs in this respect should not be denied them. This
is a question of sound policy for management and the desires of
particular groups of stockholders. No overwhelming public interest is involved. The investor who likes diversity or liquidity
will naturally put his money in a company which has imposed
such limitations on itself. There are many investors who dislike
such a company.

The people employed for the purpose, whose reputations and
livelihood depend on making good and who are directly responsible to stockholders will be far more likely to make a
success in selecting investments than will a law or regulation
by an official or commission not responsible to the stockholders
for their mistakes. Hold management accountable for misdemean-
ors but don't tie a millstone around its collective neck and expect
it to give the best results of which it is capable. There are no
investment principles so sound and changeless that they should
be imposed on management by law.

Capital profits are just as important as income to the *average*
investor in this still young and growing country. Therefore, to
require all companies to invest for income only would seem
inadvisable.

Companies should not be prevented from paying directors fair
compensation or compensating personnel on some fair profit-
sharing basis.

A law or regulation should not be too arbitrary and specific
as to the way information is presented to stockholders. Informal
clarity is better than formal confusion. An independent auditor's
certificate should be proof of accuracy. Also, I believe the English practice of having auditors elected by stockholders is a good
one.

Too much regulation will only put a premium on medi-
ocrity and a "do nothing" policy in corporate management. Care

should be taken that nothing will be set up that injects the Government without direct purpose or need into private corporate business or opens the way to harassment. If it appears that some sound public interest is involved the regulation should be limited to that necessary in the public interest.

INTRODUCTION

TO V

On December 7, 1939, I was one of four men who debated at Town Hall in New York City the question of whether government and business can effectively cooperate.

The late United States District Judge Jerome Frank, then head of the Securities and Exchange Commission, and I took the affirmative side of the question. The late Senator Robert Taft and William McChesney Martin, Jr., then head of the New York Stock Exchange but now head of the Federal Reserve Board, took the negative side.

Bureaucracy seems a necessary part of all forms of government. I have over the years done business in most of the countries of Europe and Latin America. Nowhere did I find bureaucrats more evident and powerful than in Italy, Spain and Argentina under the dictators Mussolini, Franco and Perón. They were able by delays and in other ways to blunt and thwart the desires and even the decisions of their political masters.

The trouble with our business progress in America is not that the boards, commissions and agencies are in being and functioning, because things could not be otherwise, but that they take too long with any particular case before them. Quick decisions, even if sometimes wrong, are better than perfectionist decisions that come a year or two or three too late after long, expensive and sometimes unnecessary proceedings. In business time is money. Streamlined fast-moving Bureaus, geared to finding the essentials of a case, settling it and then going on to the next case, will contribute immensely to the velocity of our national growth in business and finance.

V

~~~~~~~~~~~~~~~

I can offer myself as Exhibit *A* among living examples of regulation of business by government. During the past several years I have spent almost more time in Washington dealing with the Government than in the headquarters of the company I serve. In my attempts to steer a business course under conflicting laws, I have developed a strong feeling of sympathy for the chameleon we have all heard about. I refer to the chameleon which was dropped on a piece of Scotch plaid and burst apart trying to be all colors at the same time.

I have not burst, however. In fact, I'm so far from bursting that I can answer with an emphatic *yes* tonight's question whether government and business can effectively cooperate.

In giving that answer I don't want to be misunderstood. This has been no picnic period. I have always favored individual initiative, opportunity and freedom from restraint. For myself, I don't like regulation at any time by anyone. But as a liberal businessman, I also try to be realistic and practical. I realize that regulation is a normal relationship between government and business. I try, therefore, to help make it work smoothly and successfully.

My reason for saying that government and business can work together is rooted in my simple philosophy of business. It contains two points. One is that the economic environment of our country is dynamic, not static. The other is that business, to prosper, must accept and adapt itself to changing conditions.

Even in my lifetime business was operated on a very different basis than it is today. This early period has been referred to by some historians as the public-be-damned era. It has been referred to by some of our living elders as the good old days. Whether they were good or bad, they are gone forever. No so-called reactionaries, however much they may itch to wear the economic crowns of their fathers, can bring those days back.

Meanwhile, what is it that characterizes this new era? It is characterized both by technological and social changes. In technology we have seen the streamlined railroad and airplane conquer distance, while the radio and telephone have annihilated time.

On the social side, the aspiration level of the American people has been rapidly rising.

Both of these changes are good for business. Economically, the only way for the American people to go is upward. Anything that adds to the determination of the American people to go that way is a business asset. To provide this more abundant life is the job of business.

All this adds up to mean that the businessman no longer lives unto himself nor is a law unto himself. It also means that business and government, whether they like it or not, are obliged to draw together in a closer and closer relationship.

There can be no dispute as to whether there should be regulation. We can have a difference of opinion only as to degree.

On this there are two extreme schools of thought. One believes there should be no control—that we should return to the so-called good old days. The other believes in complete regimentation of business, even to the point of government ownership and operation. Today's papers report a statement made at last night's Congress of American Industry that America must soon face the issue as between a free competitive form of economy and government ownership. I don't believe it. Between these extremes lies the ideal in my opinion.

There are those who try to tell us that our administrators in Washington are in the extremist group, desirous of destroying private business operated for profit. I have trod the inquisitorial halls of Washington for six years and have seen no real evidence that these men are trying either to take profits out of private business or to take democracy out of government. In this statement I am naturally not referring to a small frenzied fringe of fanatics found in government and, let me add, in business too, and by whose declarations nothing can be judged.

Government impact on business naturally brings irritations. Furthermore, in the field of regulation we also have pioneering and, therefore, mistakes.

This seems to be the American way. But it is also the American way to have an umpire. We may chase the umpire off the field if he seems too partisan or engaged in making, rather than enforcing, rules. But such passing irritations do not cause us to attack the umpiring system.

I am satisfied that the great bulk of our administrators and regulators today believe that the interests of government and business go hand in hand, that the object of regulation is to help business, and that the proper object of business is to make profits.

There has also been growing evidence that regulators realize that to be good business traffic cops they don't have to—indeed, should not—sit in the driver's seat. Their function, rather, is to keep the traffic lights operating, to arrest traffic violators when practical but, above all, to keep the traffic moving as fast as possible.

The question tonight involves not only the attitude of government toward business, but equally the attitude of business toward government.

It is the job of business not only to function under regulation, but to keep regulation functioning. Business, on the defensive and openly critical, has perhaps made its own road harder than necessary. Business, by an open-minded, friendly, cooperative approach, will find itself invited by government to sit at the conference table while policies are discussed and rules formulated. I know this from experience. Every other businessman can have the same experience. It's important to be so invited, for government must learn from business itself concerning the practical problems of business. The result, I am sure, will be as welcome to government as it will be helpful to business. This, to me, is the sound substitute for the laborious and costly process of trial and error.

The thing that I worry about is not regulation or even the degree thereof. I worry much more about the attacks and counterattacks that have been going on between certain elements in government and certain elements in business these past depression years. The suspicion and fear so created caused capital to go on strike. It is the biggest strike of our lifetime, the most drawn out and the most costly. Some believe it was a lockout rather than a strike. Most of the debatable and irritating questions dealing with government and business have grown out of the efforts of government to get private capital back to work. But capital is scary. It can't be driven. It must be coaxed. Confidence is the best bait. Return of confidence, I believe, can be speeded if, among other things, business and government will declare a moratorium on name-calling and consequent breeding of suspicion. Yes, and if reforming and crusading are geared in mesh with the business profits accelerator. These beginnings will pay big dividends.

Our troubled world today needs nothing better from us than a practical home application of the good neighbor policy. Where better to begin than in the relationships between business and government? I, for one, would like to say to each "Meet a friend."

INTRODUCTION

TO VI

While serving in Washington during World War II as Director of Contract Distribution of the Office of Production Management—which was the predecessor of the War Production Board—I was called upon as part of my duties to make many speeches. My daily work was very urgent and overwhelming. Previously I had always prepared my own speeches. I had no time for such preparation during my days in Washington. The best I could do was to give to our public relations people the general thoughts I wanted to convey and let them weave such general thoughts into words to fill the allotted time. Often I would get "my" remarks as I was moving up to the rostrum.

For these reasons I include only one speech made during this period. I think it was prepared entirely by myself. I include it because it was given immediately after the Japanese attack on Pearl Harbor—on December 9, 1941, before the American Business Congress in New York City—and because it fairly clearly outlines my then task and attendant problems. Two days later, in a speech I made by telephone from Washington to the Dallas, Texas, Chamber of Commerce, the phrase "Remember Pearl Harbor" was coined.

VI

~~~~~~~~~~~~~~~~

We are now at war—total war. The man in a business suit as well as the man in uniform is now fighting the greatest battle of all time—a battle of machines, machines such as tanks and warships and planes and also machines that turn out those tanks and ships and planes.

This means the enemy will blow you out of your plant if he gets a chance. It means your plant, if it fits in with America's war program, will be a very real part of our army.

Hitler started a new kind of war. We will finish it. When he seized upon massive metal instruments of conquest, he counted too much on his six-year head start and too little on the productive capacity and will of America. Indeed, when he drew for high cards with destiny, he chose the wrong deck. We will overwhelm Hitler and his creature nations and all that they stand for with the very weight of metals.

America has said "Let's go," and the rapidly increasing tempo of production will ever increase until the job is done. We hope it will not be long. We must prepare against such a contingency.

A study of America's eighteen-month defense production record shows we have been moving fast in the right direction. Now consider the great war production effort we are starting full blast this week. Nineteen forty-two's production will be well over twice that of 1941 and the upward trend will continue into 1943 and beyond. Planning and preparation are largely over. We are ready now for all-out war production. Mountains of materials are now moving down the lines of production. We are biting in.

Because our plants can turn out more machines than those of any other nation on earth, we are the arsenal of democracy. What is this arsenal? What makes it tick? What is its pattern?

It is not concentration of production in a few plants. We have our industrial giants, it is true. They lead the way here and throughout the world in channels of commerce, and we are justly proud of them. But while they get the spotlight, they do not win a war by themselves. Beside them march thousands of little plants, the infantry of the industrial war.

Figures prove it. I'm sure I will surprise most of you by quoting some percentages: Less than one-half of one percent of our manufacturing enterprises in America employ more than 1,000 workers; less than ten percent employ more than 100 workers, and about half employ five workers or less.

Thus it is obvious that supplies for our war fronts and those for our civilian home fronts can not depend entirely on the giants any more now than they did before we went to war. Some of our armaments and most of our civilian needs must be turned out by little and medium-sized manufacturing enterprises, not by the giants alone.

This country has 200,000 factories. They are hidden away in the thousands of cities, towns and villages that dot the United States. They are our industrial life blood, the feeders of our railroads, the support of our schools and churches and civic organizations. The small plants are not merely satellites of their giant brothers. They are independent, efficient units, buying raw materials from the same sources and selling to the same customers in open competition.

We are engaged now in a war to defend our way of life. Let's be sure that in the speed of our effort, we don't overlook and lose the freedoms we are fighting to preserve. In an industrial nation

45

such as ours, industrial freedom—preservation of our pattern—must be one of them. I speak of it particularly tonight because my phase of the war effort concerns this industrial field, and at this moment I am addressing the medium-sized and small manufacturers.

When the small factories of America die or become merely subordinate units in major groups controlled at the top, I say many other things we are fighting to defend will also die.

As an early move in Germany's industrial mobilization, Hitler closed up more than 20,000 little factories and moved their workers and machinery into the bigger plants. That fitted the Nazi pattern and philosophy. It must not happen here.

While mobilizing our industrial resources, we must not be shortsighted. We must keep one clear eye on the postwar problem—and by the same token one protecting hand on small manufacturers and the communal life they foster. For, indeed, we can not spare or replace them, either in peace or in war.

President Roosevelt gave me orders last September to help mobilize industry. This is the way I interpret his command: Industry is to be mobilized with the immediate and urgent task of all-out war production particularly in mind. But an accent must be placed on helping small business and its workers to avoid the harmful effects of raw materials shortages.

I believe heart and soul in the need for this accent in the President's order.

We need our industrial giants in war production. They are well qualified on their own to lead America's armaments race and to keep their workers and plants busy in the process. They don't need my help. I need theirs and I'm thankful to say I'm getting it in no small measure. But America also needs the little fellow's help, and he needs ours. He will get it to the best of my ability and to the full limit of my authority.

We are pitted against nations that have been long using unlimited governmental power to organize their economies for aggression. For years they have been at it, fitting each factory craftily and ruthlessly into the job it could do best for the war front or the home front.

Against industrial forces so organized, we must quickly bring to bear our utmost industrial strength. That does not mean putting all plants into armaments. It means selective mobilization—war production in industries best suited to it and essential civilian output in factories adapted to that vital role.

We are producing for the military establishment at a rate absorbing about one quarter of our national income. Our production for the men who are fighting our battles on land and sea and in the air must now climb swiftly. We must use all the arms-producing capacity we can without impairing the health and efficiency of the workers, the farmers, the businessmen, the housewives who back up the fighting front. To do less than that would betray our men at arms and invite national disaster.

But even when our war production absorbs nearly half our national income, as it must and shall, that effort will require only about half our total productive capacity. There will be another half left over to produce essential civilian goods to the full extent that raw materials are available for that purpose.

We can turn out about $100,000,000,000 worth of goods a year if we have the raw materials to do it. We have the plants, and the labor to make them hum. The only bottleneck is the supply of scarce materials, which must be used where they will contribute most to the nation's fighting power.

Just as all military personnel can't be in the cockpit of a fighting plane, all industry can't turn out munitions. Each must do the part he can do best.

Some machines can work to fine tolerances and some can't. Some work requires fine tolerances and some doesn't. It is wasteful for a machine that can do precision work on the weapons we need to be working on civilian products where precision is not required. And it is just as wasteful for a plant most useful in civilian fields to undertake intricate precision work on armaments. Indeed, it will be tragic if our production is slowed down and plants are forced out of business as a result of such blunders.

Many of the smaller plants can do precision work, but generally speaking, the greatest and most quickly available reservoir of unused arms-making capacity is in the larger and medium-sized factories.

What we must do is determine the natural role of each factory, large and small, and mobilize them accordingly as fast as possible. Most of you know from experience how hard it is to mobilize one small plant and keep it busy. I know, too, for I have had that personal problem.

Well, then, consider the task of mobilizing our 200,000 plants. Of these, 133,000 are little ones and employ only twenty people or less. Without an over-all policy and an orderly approach, thousands of very small factories will die of material shortages before we can reach them and decide what they should do.

My plan is simply this: I want the responsible officials to grant small factories enough scarce raw materials to keep them going on a skeletonized basis during the next six months. Speaking generally, two percent of the total supply of these materials will keep them alive until we can reach them on a plant-by-plant basis. Naturally, this cannot be applied to some rare materials all needed for defense.

Small plants receiving fair offers of defense work during this period would be required to accept them, or suffer reductions in their allowances of materials.

In the meantime, we would be free to concentrate upon the conversion of more of the larger and medium-sized plants from civilian to arms work. It is in this field that the available manpower can bring about the greatest possible increase in arms output in the shortest possible time.

Rumor has it that my plan has provoked violent controversy with my associates in the Office of Production Management. I believe there is no one in the OPM who wants to hurt little business. Everyone would like to see small business kept alive if it can be done without crippling our military effort.

This proposal for small business seems to me to be the best and perhaps the only way to keep our economic highways from being cluttered with needless wreckage. I believe the responsible officials will approve it at least as to its essentials. But whether or not they see their way clear to adopting this program, I will carry on, continuing my efforts to convert qualified plants to arms production as quickly as possible. I know that little business also will accept whatever over-all policy is found necessary in this grave hour.

If the plan to grant small plants a limited amount of scarce materials were adopted, the task of administering it would admittedly be difficult. Success would depend on the cooperation it received from small business itself. And while success might mean prolongation of the plan, failure would mean an end to it and the development of a new small business problem fraught with harmful consequences.

Failure could come only in case small businesses used more scarce materials than we contemplate. They could not be permitted to cut into the supply for direct and indirect war needs. They could not use all of the remainder available for civilian production, because there are other plants to be considered too.

Never before have we needed more pulling together than right now. Never before have we had more opportunity to serve or a greater necessity to forget selfish interests. Already, with the products of American industry, a chain of aluminum and copper and steel is being drawn around the mechanical monsters that Germany and Japan have turned loose against the civilized world. At some points the chain is already so close that Hitler can hear the rattle of its links—for him a death rattle. His requiem will be sung by the pistons of our plants; his black shroud will come from our belching smokestacks.

Only then can we have peace and justice for all.

INTRODUCTION

to VII

Shortly after Pearl Harbor I agreed to deliver the commencement address, in May 1942, at Hillsdale College, Michigan. I had finished high school in Hillsdale, while my sister and one of my brothers were attending the college. At the time of this address I was still serving as a director of the Office of Production Management, although I was at a low physical ebb as a result of an onslaught of rheumatoid arthritis which subsequently forced me to resign the post.

I agreed to deliver this address because I thought that I had some special and worth-while thoughts to express to the youngsters who were graduating into a war-torn world—a world that would face them with new postwar problems. In rereading this address eighteen years later I believe I forecast those problems fairly accurately.

VII

~~~~~~~~~~~~~~~~

You of the graduating class assemble during this quiet hour in observance of a tradition as ancient as institutions of learning. It is an hour of congratulation for tasks completed; of contemplation of those moral and spiritual precepts germane to the soul of man which should motivate his activities; an hour of communion and benediction.

I often think back to that June day in 1914 when, as a senior at the University of Colorado, I listened to my *last* baccalaureate address.

How swift has been the march of events since my commencement! Such change is worth noting, for I believe it has a rather direct bearing on the trouble and confusion that now surround us. Then we had no radio, and the airplane was just making its first appearance. The automobile was still a novelty. The telephone was something to be treated with respect and used only on special occasions. China, India and Russia were faraway places, inhabited by peoples whose activities were remote from ours, and heard about seldom and then usually many weeks after the event. In a word, the earth has grown smaller rapidly in terms of time and space, and all the peoples of the earth have suddenly become neighbors familiar almost instantly with details of each other's lives. The development of the machine and mass production have brought blessings to some, while others, less fortunate, have come to focus on that happy picture and have learned to envy. Envy breeds covetousness. The machine, developed to help us to higher standards of living, becomes, in the hands of the envious and avaricious, an instrument for destruction and conquest. The "have nots" are on the march to take from those who have. And there are "have nots" measured by whole races and nations. The same forces have always been at work. But wireless and airplane have brought us to a frenzied tempo involving everyone.

My generation fought a war to make the world safe for democracy. We did not succeed. Out of the ruins of that struggle arose a multi-headed monster more rapacious than the old, and in the stench were bred strange philosophies dangerous to us and our desired ways of life. We are now in a new death struggle to preserve our heritage. Uncounted millions of specialized murderers, armed with every device of destruction that science can devise, directed by unbridled overlords, are waging war against us. Ruthless carnage and destruction pursue their relentless way on land, on sea, and in the air.

Hitler's forces started this war to get what others have, by extermination and subjugation. Terror and destruction are by sadistic plan. Note the horrible suffering, and view the long lines of trenches of unmarked graves in Poland and in Greece. In the East mark the slimy path of Japan along the Asiatic coast and the thousands upon thousands of civilian Chinese who have been methodically massacred, simply as a warning to their kindred that the invaders will tolerate no restraint and that their rule shall be supreme. Consider the lightning-like stroke of the aggressors' poisonous fangs—Pearl Harbor, the Philippines, Singapore and elsewhere. These demonstrate, beyond all doubt, the execution of a plan of systematic pillage and conquest, not newborn but of long duration and requiring years of treacherous diplomacy and careful preparation for their sudden unfolding. Germany planned and worked from 1933 with but one object in mind; Japan from 1930. When Hitler's hordes moved into Poland, they were backed by a hundred-billion-dollar war machine and industrial activity was at its peak.

Only now, for the first time, does the combined war production of Russia, Britain and the United States equal that of the Axis powers. No wonder we have seen a succession of reverses. We must steel our hearts against the possibility of further misfortune until our machine and manpower have built up a surplus with which to overwhelm our enemies. You will be actively contributing to that effort from now on. Our productive effort, although already great, must be still greater. Our call on tools and personnel for the normal things of peaceful life must be kept to the minimum to release hands and machines for the critical, urgent military effort. There can be no idle hands. If we falter in our efforts to arm and train, if we lag in the production of guns, tanks, ships and planes, if we fail to furnish food, clothing and the innumerable other things required in total war, we —each one of us—may suffer the grinding pain of the conqueror's heel. You have an immediate task.

The results to us of a defeat by such forces are almost impossible to comprehend. Certain it is, however, that our form of government would largely disappear. "Freedom of speech and expression, religious freedom, freedom from want and freedom from fear" would exist only as a memory. Individual rights and self-expression and their gracious consorts, happiness and contentment, would wither and die; their joyous offspring, literature, music and the arts, would fade and decline and but haltingly mutter the doleful sounds and lamentations of an oppressed people. History would roll back on itself nearly to its beginnings, more Stygian in its blackness than the Dark Ages.

If I have stated what seem to be extreme views, it is because I believe we are engaged in the most horrible war mankind has ever been called upon to endure. It is universal and total. It affects civilians and soldiers alike. The principles we have held to be axiomatic and inalienable may be wrenched from our lives and lost. The Declaration of Independence announced these precepts as the lodestar of our existence. The Constitution and Bill of Rights was a solemn covenant by our forefathers that those fundamental rights should never be denied or withdrawn. If we lose them now, can it be said that life is worth living? There is but one course to follow.

Every energy we possess, every resource we can control should be devoted to the single purpose of winning the war. The desire to win must be vitalized and made the dominant factor in all our activities. We have social, economic and political problems, but their solution is of minor importance until we have gained a peace through victory. Total war means total participation. Whether one is called to combat service, to man merchant ships at sea, to build planes or tanks, to raise the crops, prepare the food, nurse the wounded or stand watch through the lonely nights, it is service demanding loyalty and constant application to the task; all are essential to the functioning of the common cause. There can be no shifting of responsibility or failure to participate. Although the burdens assumed may differ, the results of defeat will fall alike on all, regardless of the parts taken by each. My neighbor has a right to demand that I serve; he likewise owes a duty to you and to me. It's a one-way road, an uphill road with no free rides. There is an immediate task awaiting you.

My firm belief in our ultimate victory is grounded in my faith in the capacity of the American people. In times of peace we are inclined to shirk our public duty, criticize those who seek to serve, waste our energies in trivial affairs, shift our responsibilities and, through pressure groups and organizations, seek favors which may be contrary to the common good. But in emergencies or when the call to duty has been clear and understood, never yet have we failed. Never yet have freedom's children forsaken her in her hour of trial, nor will they falter now. From Iceland and Australia, from Alaska and Panama, from Ireland and the islands of the Pacific, from a hundred camps within our shores, from our ships on all the seas, we hear but one reply: "We are ready." From farm and hamlet, city and village, mountain and plain, from homes, ships, schools and colleges, we echo the cry: "Here am I, send me." That includes you—the class of 1942.

I deeply regret that I cannot speak to you today of less somber matters, on subjects traditionally associated with occasions of this nature. It would be pleasant to go forward in fancy with you, radiant in the garments of your completed scholastic training, pulsating with clear purpose and high ambitions, as normally you would go, each to his chosen field without hindrance from others; to lay the pattern of your lives as seems to you right or desirable; there to make your homes and weave the fabric of your own affairs, free men in a free country. These are entertaining vistas, but the journey must await the return of happier times.

We hear much today about special privilege and the unfair distribution of this and that and the other thing. This is nothing new. It is not altogether man-made. To the extent that it can be bettered with justice, it should be bettered. Whatever can be argued about the fairness or unfairness of unequal distribution, one thing must stand out unchallenged, namely, that the privileged have a duty to use their resources as best they can for the good of society as a whole.

And you are among the specially privileged. You have been privileged in a most outstanding way in the matter of education. You must use this training, which has been denied the many others, to lead the way and to help. You have assumed an obligation to demonstrate to the society that made such privilege possible that your student days have not been fruitless. As you have learned to recognize those fundamental human values without which education is barren, yours is the responsibility to cherish and preserve them. To choose your life course and field of work as you desire, to enjoy the beauties and inspiration of nature and the arts freely, to read, to think, to express yourselves without coercion save only the dictates of conscience, to worship as your hearts incline, to marry as you love, to preserve one's personality with dignity and honor—these things are among those fundamental human values. Of these things you have learned while you have been absorbing facts, figures, formulas and philosophies. The right to enjoy these things is the heritage only for a free people. They came to you through the toil, the sweat, the blood and the suffering of your forefathers. They must be preserved the same way and vouchsafed to you and your children's children by a great society of free people—this democracy of ours. You face a more difficult task, a more dangerous future, a greater duty and responsibility than has ever before confronted any graduate since the birth of this nation. Never before have those cherished rights and aspirations, those essential liberties, without which life holds no happiness, been in such jeopardy.

The cessation of actual war will not bring you rest from your labors or relief from your responsibilities. The peace treaty will usher in a period of adjustment and reconstruction that will be difficult in the extreme. There will be a new concept of social relationships to analyze. There will be new political philosophies. The old economic foundations upon which we relied before the war will be gone. New superstructures of society, trade and finance will have to be built. It will be your task to see that they are not built on quicksand.

Our greater productive capacity created for war effort must be absorbed in greater demands and higher standards of living, or unemployment and distress will result. The answer must be found to the problem of man's leisure. Man has created machines which have created more time for leisure. Let's not be engulfed by our own creation. Let's remain the masters of our destiny.

I'll count on you to do your part. I'll hope to look back with pride on your efforts, on your proof that education does pay dividends in terms of sound leadership that cannot be swayed by day-to-day emotions and economic claptrap but carries through to a sounder and better democratic society. It is your duty to become leaders. That means education must be made the tool of intelligence. That means you must win and justify confidence; you must separate the mental and emotional wheat from the chaff; you must be able to view each problem from the other side as well as your own, and know how to energize deliberation into action and how to become a part of the spearhead of sound public opinion.

I do not expect you to solve all the problems completely, for problems are ever present. Each milepost in the progress of the human race brings new problems, new adjustments. The task is to bring the relation of man to man and race to race as nearly as possible into harmony with the existing state of progress and knowledge. To find the task completed would, I fear, be to realize that progress has stagnated. The flight of man is endless. Each goal is but a resting place for the night. In this endless flight we need, as our navigation instruments, wisdom, temperance and justice. For fuel we need courage, ambition and knowledge.

Your schooling, now completed, may seem to have lost some of its applicable value when considering some of the tasks immediately before you. But this won't be true. What you have absorbed will serve its useful purpose in the immediate future as well as after peace. This schooling has become a part of you. Remember that education and civilization have marched hand in hand down the centuries, neither capable of existence without the other. Wherever they have dwelt together, man has become finer and nobler. Institutions have appeared for the betterment of mankind; ideals of liberty, freedom and justice have flourished; peace, joy and happiness have blossomed; music has charmed the ear, literature has lent its fantasy to the leisure hours and art has delighted the eye.

Nowhere in all the world has man prospered so well and reaped such abundant harvests as in this land of ours—this land and its institutions which belong to all of us, irrespective of race or creed. As a boy I heard a poem. I don't know who wrote it, but the substance has stuck with me throughout the years:

> America mine! Aye, comrades, and thine,
> Thine, from England, from Africa's plains,
> From the fair lands of Egypt, Austria, Spain,
> Here on the sod under night's pall,
> I cry out, thank God,
> For it's free, and for me and for thee,
> The fairest, the rarest that man ever trod,
> The sweetest, the dearest
> 'Twixt the sky and the sod.
> And it's mine and it's thine, thank God.

Let's keep that fair land and its institutions free and untarnished for ourselves and our progeny. The fortitude of Valley Forge has gained new luster in crushed Bataan. Corregidor and the Coral Sea are equally outstanding accomplishments. Our people will never fail us. You are a part of that people now about to assume your burdens. Keep ever in mind what good citizenship and sound leadership mean. And God be with you.

INTRODUCTION

TO VIII

World War II started our country on an inflationary course. In my annual report to stockholders of Atlas Corporation for the year 1942 I considered it advisable to discuss the subject of inflation. Such discussion follows as Number VIII in this book.

This original presentation was by no means complete. Following that original statement are some remarks that I made on the same subject in 1957. The two should be read together.

VIII

~~~~~~~~~~~~~~~~~~

(1942)

The word *inflation* causes most of us to think of conditions in Germany during and following World War I when money there kept shrinking in value, with resulting skyrocketing prices, until in 1923 it took about 240 billions of dollars valued in prewar marks to buy a dozen eggs. We know that the German astronomical price inflation was due to deliberate uncontrolled feeding out of "printing press" money, rather than to an undue shortage of goods, eggs in this instance.

The United States, too, had inflation during World War I, but here it was due to other causes than unsound currency and only resulted in eggs going up from 20¢ a dozen to 60¢. We had another inflationary period during the twenties which ended in the crash of late 1929 and resulted in the subsequent depression. But in this second inflationary period we saw different causal factors at work and different results in various segments of our national economy. For example: between 1914 and 1920 wages increased about 2¼ times, the cost of living increased about 2 times and industrial stock prices increased about 1⅔ times; but, from 1924 to 1929 we saw wages increase by only 7 percent, the cost of living not at all, while industrial stock prices advanced about 3 times.

We must realize, therefore, that inflation does not always follow the same pattern.

Factors tending toward inflation are again at work in this country and have been for some time past. However, indications are that they may be checked and controlled to the point that they may not have as much inflationary effect as during the last war, even though our national war effort and its effect at that time on our economy were small compared with our present all-out effort.

Inflation has to do with money and price of things available for purchase. Money is purely a medium of exchange and has no particular value apart from the things that it will buy now or in the future.

The value of money, as represented by the quantity of goods or services it will obtain, is expressed in prices. The unit of money, which is one dollar, remains the same but prices for things fluctuate. If one commodity or only a few rise in price, this is usually due to a shortage of such commodity or commodities and the rise usually brings into the market a greater supply of the particular items and causes the situation to stabilize itself. But if there is a general price rise in all commodities so that in each case it takes more dollars to buy the commodity but nevertheless the owner of one bushel of wheat can get the same amount of fruit or eggs or milk for it as he did before, then it is the dollar that has fallen in value rather than the wheat that has increased.

As long as money (representing buying power) and the quantity of goods available for purchase remain in normal relationship to each other, a stable price level results. If either half of the relationship gets out of normal balance with the other we have a change in price levels.

If the goods and services available at a given price exceed the ability of consumers to purchase them, prices drop and we have deflation. Inflation exists when prices rise because there is too much spending power in the hands of the people for the volume of goods and services available for purchase.

A large and rapid rise in general prices, representing as it does a change in the purchasing power of money, has a bad dislocating effect in that it distorts one segment of our economy in relation to another.

The person who has saved up future purchasing power has lost a part of such savings. This is true whether he left the money in the form of cash in bank or loaned it out or bought annuities or bonds or life insurance. What he gets back from these fixed repayments of dollars will buy less.

The company that has borrowed lots of money through a bond issue can pay it off with less product of its plant than contemplated when the loan was made and is at an advantage over a perhaps more conservative competitor. The company that has committed ahead for sale of products finds its costs have risen so its profit has disappeared at the stipulated sale price.

The wage or salary earner must get more dollars for his work or he will be getting less, for with his old wage he can buy fewer necessities and comforts.

In other words, the effect of inflation is to distort and to cause values arbitrarily to shift from one class or group or individual to another.

Because inflation hits most people at the point of daily necessities, President Roosevelt, in his public discussions of the subject, has chosen to use "Rise in Cost of Living" instead of "inflation."

War has always a strong tendency to carry inflation in its wake. That is because it causes both sides of the relationship between consumer purchasing power and things available for purchase to be violently changed.

War brings the Government into the market with an urgent need for goods and the means of making them. It demands goods faster than they can be made and this very urgency tends to pull prices upward. The tremendous output of war goods and corresponding outpouring of purchasing power in the hands of the people continues until military victory is won.

In the early stages the Government is generally in competition with civilians for goods—or at least for the materials and facilities necessary to produce goods. The Government buys all it can and the civilians, having more income and spendable money in hand, also buy more. This pull on prices finds a push helping it too, for prices are also forced upward by increased costs of production of which increased labor cost is only a part.

In this period just referred to the nation is trying to make "both guns and butter." That is to say, it is trying through increased production not only to meet the demands of the Armed Services, but the increased demands of civilians as well. Of course, the realization that this cannot be done because of insufficient man-power, materials and facilities is soon reached and there begins a transition period where there is much more defense work and reduced supplies of some things for civilians. Then comes the final period when we go to the limit of war production, which means cutting supplies for civilian consumption to bare bones.

In this country the first phase lasted until toward the middle of 1941, the second period lasted until the end of 1941 or a little beyond, since which time we have been rapidly running the course of the final all-out period.

The danger of inflation starts only in the second period, for until then the civilian finds plenty of things to buy with his additional spending power.

The total value of all goods and services produced by our national economy (known as the Gross National Product) expanded greatly between the low point in the depression and 1942. But notwithstanding this and increased individual incomes there was available for civilian consumption in 1942 less than in 1941 and there will be even less so available in 1943.

This shortage of goods for the civilian gives us one side of the equation that, when uncontrolled, has inflation as the answer. We have less things that we are financially able to buy.

The other side of the equation is the purchasing power available in relation to the goods available for purchase. The Gross

National Expenditure and its breakdown shows this buying power increasing enormously. The excess of available funds to purchase goods over available goods for purchase has increased from about 8 billion dollars in 1940 to over 26 billion dollars in 1942 and will be in excess of 40 billion dollars for 1943.

The spread between purchasing power and things to buy, minus probable individual normal savings, represents what the public officials refer to as the inflationary gap.

The pressure of this excess buying power on prices would be terrific and would be sure to bring us into an inflationary spiral if things were allowed to take their normal uncontrolled course.

But they are not being allowed to take their normal course.

The President, on April 27, 1942, in his message to Congress said: "The time has definitely come to stop the spiral and we can face the fact that there must be a drastic reduction in our standard of living."

Now let us see how far the inflationary movement had progressed when the President thus spoke.

Since August 1939 (just before the war started) the hourly wage had gone up about one third and the weekly effective wage (due to overtime) over 50 percent; non-farm prices had gone up about one fourth while farm prices had gone up three quarters. The cost of living had gone up 18 percent and farm real estate prices had gone up about 8 percent. During the same period industrial stock prices actually decreased by about 22 percent.

While there had been considerable action directed to holding many prices down prior to the fall of 1942 the problems had not been met head on. This was particularly true in the matter of wages and farm prices. And in relation to the different and more vigorous approach in the fall of 1942 it is of interest and importance to remember that the President, throughout the depression years, set as his goal the re-establishment of the 1926 general level of prices as normal, and that this level has now been reached.

The movement back from the depression lows to normal could not be considered inflation. Inflationary tendencies until last fall had merely speeded up return to what was considered normal. At that time the Government took positive steps to prevent so far as possible, by law and administrative power, the effect of competitive pressure of excess buying power on prices.

Reflecting the increasing shortage of things to buy, rationing came more and more into force, but is yet only a promise of what is to come. The purpose of rationing is to see that the inadequate supplies of civilian goods are divided equitably. If the bread must be spread thinly, then the purpose is to see that it is spread evenly.

The Government had been fighting inflation in other ways. The problem can be approached by either reducing the spendable money or increasing civilian goods. Inasmuch as the latter alternative is impossible, the Administration tackled the spendable money end of the problem.

To the extent that the people save this excess purchasing power, it has no present inflationary influence. To the extent that the Government takes this excess in taxes, it is not available for private spending.

The Government has been trying both methods. It has increased taxes and proposes to increase them again. And it has carried on an intensive campaign to get the people to buy United States War Bonds and Stamps. Most of the inflationary gap is being absorbed in these ways. Savings are increasing fast.

The Government, believing that it would not be safe to assume that the people will voluntarily save all these more than 40 billion dollars expected to be available for that purpose in 1943, proposes to make sure that a large part of this money will, in any event, be sterilized so far as pressure on goods and prices is concerned.

It is proposed to take part of this excess in increased taxes and a part of the remainder in forced savings, that is to say, it will take it as a tax but return it after the war in certain installments.

Such a program, if carried out completely and vigorously to cover all the savings, would prevent inflation. The people would not have any money to spend over and above what there is available to buy.

And in return for the resulting Spartan existence with all its hardships, there might be offered a sound economy when peace comes.

But there is no proposal to take all this excess spending power in taxes and forced savings; and no assurance that the remainder not so taken will go into War Bonds or other forms of savings so that it will not be offered competitively for goods.

Also, absolute controls are very difficult under our democratic form of government. The industrial laborer does not want inflation, but he wants a higher wage. The farmer does not want inflation, but he wants higher prices for his product. The businessman does not want inflation, but he wants to make more profits.

And so the pressure groups develop, and the proposals to control inflation lead to a series of compromises and less than completely all-out measures. The net result is that price increases are slowed down to a walk rather than a run.

There has been a great deal of discussion on how national income is being distributed under prevailing war conditions. Without becoming a party to the discussion, it must be pointed out that the very large increase in wages as well as the number of wage-earners suggests that the middle-income group, from $1,750 to $10,000 per year, has expanded very markedly. The National Bureau of Economic Research estimated that, based on a hypothetical Net National Income of 109 billions for the fiscal year 1943 (expressed in 1940 dollars), distribution would be about 18% to people with incomes of $1,750 and below, about 18% to people with incomes of $10,000 and over, and the remaining about 73% to people with incomes between $1,750 and $10,000.

The main point, so far as present discussion is concerned, is that any fiscal measure which is effectively to deal with this problem of price control must recognize the enormous purchasing power lodged with the middle group. It is evident that a considerable portion of the inflationary gap rests in the brackets of incomes between $1,750 and $10,000.

During 1942 a large amount was "saved" in that it was not spent for goods or services. But perhaps a part of it was only considered set aside for spending in the comparatively near future, in which event its pressure on prices could only be said to be postponed.

Any tax or forced savings law that does not have its greatest impact on individuals with incomes between $1,750 and $10,000 will fail in its purpose. Such a law will reach well over 21 million heads of families or single people living and acting as an economic unit. It need not touch, to any effective degree, the nearly 20 millions more with incomes below $1,750. There are fewer than 1 million economic units with incomes over $10,000.

So far as control of inflation is concerned a "forced savings" tax measure can allow many deductions that are not permitted for regular income tax purposes. An individual expenditure that by its nature does not place any appreciable pressure on limited goods or prices can properly be allowed, and in many cases should be, to avoid hardship. Payments for education, or support of relatives, or for charities, or insurance, or in reduction of debts are cited as examples.

(Additional Remarks in 1957)

The decline of the dollar in recent years is certainly inflation. The whole subject of inflation, its causes and effects, is most complicated and technical. But inflation is what President Eisenhower has recently stated to be our greatest present internal national problem. It's what caused interest rates to be increased recently. And interest rates and inflationary movements have a great deal to do with the course of stock and bond market prices.

Such inflation as we have been experiencing in this country—an annual average of about 3 percent since 1939—is, as already indicated, due to a combination of many complex factors.

The Government has spent the 273 billion dollars that it now owes as national debt, plus all that it has taken in through taxes. And these large expenditures, most of which were for goods and services, play a great part in inflation, particularly in war times or times of heavy national defense when so many people are in the Armed Services and therefore out of productive employment, and when such a large portion of the national product is being taken by the Government.

It is interesting to note how our national debt has grown. After the Civil War it amounted to $78 per person. After World War I it was about $240 per person. Today it is about $1,600 per person. Our national debt was about 41 percent of the national income after World War I and it is about 77 percent of national income today. This is only our national debt of about 273 billion dollars. The state debt would bring this total public debt up to about 312 billion dollars or to about 88 percent of national income.

Is it any wonder that with this enormous expenditure by the Government, taxes have increased out of proportion to increase in income or increase in population? During the last thirty-three years our population has increased by 50 percent but Federal income taxes have gone up about 1,400 percent.

There is one thing that should be borne in mind in connection with our system of income taxes. The Government can meet its present-size budget only if the present level of business prosperity is maintained. If corporate and business profits were to recede to any substantial extent the Government would be faced with deficit financing.

Wages for labor can have a direct bearing on the inflationary spiral. Wage increases, when not offset by increased productivity or other economies, increase the cost of production and therefore represent an inflationary push from the bottom. But we are in a period of great technological advances—the so-called machine age in which the horsepower or kilowatt is taking over the job previously done by human hand and foot. Mechanics are substituting for muscle. When there is an increase in productivity sufficient to offset the increase in wages, plus the investment and operating costs incident to the machinery that has been added to obtain that increased productivity, there is no net inflationary push. In fact the net effect could be a reduction of costs with a consequent possible reduction of prices.

The major long-term upward trend is due in part to growth of population but also in part to increased output per man hour through increased use of mechanical energy. For the long period since 1909 the increase in hourly wages has averaged about 5.6 percent per year while output or productivity per man hour has increased an average of only 2.7 percent per year. The difference between these two percentages of about 3 percent per year compares with an average inflation or falling purchasing value of the dollar during the same period of about 1 percent. Since the start of World War II the increase of hourly wages has averaged about 6.8 percent while the productivity per man hour has fallen away from its previous trend and has increased an average of about 1.6 percent per year. The difference between the two is about 5.2 percent. The dollar during the same period has lost an average of about 3 percent per year in purchasing power.

While this has some evidential bearing on the complex of impacts that result in inflation, I am not intending to suggest that wages are too high. I am intending to suggest that productivity per man hour is too low. By increasing this productivity fast enough wage scales can still point upward with no harm and perhaps with much good. We can increase this productivity by more intensified use of machine and mechanical energy. Thus a great inflationary push from the bottom can be eliminated. We should work the machines in place to their full capacity. An increase in wages, if accompanied by increase in productivity to offset the increased items of cost, both of man and machine, seems to me wholesome because it brings about more disposable income, a higher standard of living and a beneficial effect on business activity.

The cheaper and more widespread the use of mechanical energy, the more labor can earn and for fewer hours of work. That is where atomic energy will play a great role in the future. It will make more abundant the supply of heat and mechanical energy while keeping the cost of same down to or below present levels. Check the various countries of the world, as I have, and you will find that prosperity does not come with or from low wages, but that the amount of mechanical energy used per capita is a true yardstick of national prosperity and standard of living. We in the United States are using more and more mechanical power. At the turn of the century we had available mechanical energy of about ½ horsepower per capita. Today we have about 50 horsepower of mechanical energy per capita and in consequence we lead the world in output, wages and standard of living. A horsepower is the energy required to raise 33,000 pounds of weight one foot in one minute. Every minute in the day every person in this country has available to him enough mechanical pushbutton power to raise 800 tons one foot. Less human work for more pay will come from using this availability of mechanical energy to the limit and by increasing the amount available. A kilowatt does not require food, clothes, sleep or amusement.

Before dropping this subject I would like to say just one thing more. Since 1939 the number of people in our civilian labor force has increased by about 40 percent, our gross national product in terms of a constant dollar has increased by about 100 percent, our productivity per man hour has increased about 45 percent, and average wages per man hour, while they have increased from 63¢ to over $2.00, only absorb in the aggregate 32 percent of our gross national product now, whereas they absorbed about 46 percent of such gross national product in 1939. Again this indicates to me that increasing productivity per man through use of mechanical energy is perhaps the principal solution to our problem of inflation. . . .

INTRODUCTION

to IX

I have always enjoyed the luxury of being an independent in politics. This means that my vote has shifted from one major party to the other depending on my opinion at the given time of the candidates and party pledges.

For a considerable time I sat on the Board of Governors of Town Hall. One of my fellow governors was Norman Thomas, the Socialist party's candidate for President on several occasions. He was an intelligent, likable man but considered a rank radical at the time. How far this nation of ours has moved to the left is evidenced by the fact that practically all the major planks in the platform of the Socialist party headed by Norman Thomas have since been adopted by our Republican and Democratic parties.

In December 1948 I was called upon to make the principal address at a dinner at the Waldorf-Astoria Hotel to honor the Honorable Alben W. Barkley, then Vice President-elect of the United States. I still stand by the remarks I made on that occasion, which accompany this preface.

IX

~~~~~~~~~~~~~~~~~~~~~~

I am a living example—said to be a rarity—of how to be a
farmer, a Democrat, a glutton of privilege and happy all at the
same time.

I can remain happy even while contemplating the growing
voice of labor for a little larger piece of the national pie. It's a
very big pie. And I can remain a Democrat while still differing
with some of the views of my good friend Senator O'Mahoney,
with whom I worked in the newspaper field out in Colorado more
than thirty years ago.

I have been carefully studying indicative national figures recently and I would like to generalize about some of them in what
might be called headline fashion.

While employees today have slightly less of the national income percentagewise than they had last year or had on the average during the last ten years, they have more in dollars than
ever before. Neither of these statements tells the whole story,
however, because the dollar which they are getting more of is in-
flated but, on the other hand, if corporate profits should go down
to nothing as they did in 1932, the compensation of employees
in percentage of the national income would go away up notwithstanding great unemployment and suffering. To draw a real
conclusion as to fair division of the dollars of private business

enterprises one must have a view as to the permanency of present levels of business profits.

Senator O'Mahoney and others have expressed the view that through an excess profits tax, through price reductions and in other ways, corporate profits should be reduced. I affirm that both corporate employees and the United States Government have too great a stake in corporate profits to let them recede. A few facts will make this apparent.

If business is a gamble, then Uncle Sam is the greatest gambler in history, for he rakes in about fifty percent of everything that corporations have left after expense of operations. Uncle Sam gets part of this by direct corporate profits tax and part as a tax on shareholders when they receive their dividends.

Not only this, but nearly half of all that Uncle Sam gets to live on comes from the same corporations by way of these taxes on profits and dividends.

It is beyond argument that in these prosperous times the Government must have a surplus to apply to debt reduction. It is still debatable whether for the current and forthcoming fiscal years the Government will or will not need more taxes to accomplish this necessary result. I can tell you for sure, however, that this depends on whether corporate profits stay up. A 15 percent drop in corporate profits would mean a loss to the Government in tax revenues of more than two billion dollars and would make a deficit a certainty. The Government has adopted a system of taxation that ties the Government's financial stability to a high level of corporate profits. If you are going to worry about the future of corporate profits, then also start worrying even more about the finances of your Government.

And if corporate profits are going to be reduced by drop in prices and rise in wages by say 25 percent, where is the Government going to make up the loss of about four billion dollars in taxes?

The law of diminishing returns tells me that the Government

cannot get more out of the higher individual income brackets. That is one law that even Congress can't repeal. Every person's income in excess of say $50,000 could be confiscated and this would not begin to make up the difference.

The platform of the Democratic party seems to tell me that the difference won't be made up by a higher rate on smaller incomes.

That leaves an increased tax on corporations as the probable alternative.

So I say get more taxes from earnings of corporations if greater Government revenues are necessary. Also avoid further inflation by all proper means, give employees their full, fair share of the national income, but let's for our own national sake do nothing to interfere with the soundness of health and the business activity of our corporate tax collecting slaves.

I was always taught by my father that more flies can be caught with sugar than with vinegar. If I could show a way to get more Government revenues by actually reducing rather than raising taxes, it would be a neat trick, you must admit. I think I can do this, and without the aid of illusion or mirrors. The magic unfolds itself in steps.

Common stocks are about the only thing that have not responded proportionately to the decreased value of the dollar, better known as inflation. Common stocks have gone down greatly since 1929 while everything else has gone up greatly. Common stocks are selling so low today in relation to either earnings or dividends that companies cannot afford to issue more stock to get the cash needed for capital requirements. In consequence, corporations are holding back earnings and using the same for plant additions. To the extent that earnings won't suffice, these corporations are to a large extent borrowing money. Why are common stocks selling at such a discount? In my opinion it is not because of fear of depression, but because there is too little left for investors out of corporate earnings after all taxes are taken out, to make the purchase of stocks worth while at anything short of a heavy discount. A corporation that is earning 20 percent on its invested capital before taxes is definitely on a prosperity basis. Yet, if that corporation should pay its taxes and declare out as dividends 40 percent of what is left, a recipient who is in the highest income brackets would have less than 1 percent left for himself as return on that portion of the company's capital that he has contributed. You can be sure that such a man will normally seek either a higher return by buying such a company's stock at forty or fifty cents on the dollar, or a more sure return, or a tax-free income, rather than take 1 percent. Even the man of middle income would have less than 3 percent left in the corporate example cited.

I now affirm that if stockholders were given a credit against taxes otherwise payable by them of some part of the dividends received, so that even at worst a high-income-bracket stockholder would end up with more than obtainable by him from a tax-free municipal bond, the following would happen: Stocks would rise. Corporations would sell common stock to finance capital additions. Thus, earnings now retained would be freed for dividends. The Government, while not taking more than 70 or 80 percent of the dividend in any particular case, would get much more in aggregate dollars than it now gets from taxes on dividends.

If by such a sugar rather than vinegar process of catching golden flies, corporations could pay out 70 percent of earnings as they once did rather than less than 40 percent as they do now, the Government would get upward of two billion dollars of additional income taxes. As I originally said, by tax rate reductions with no tax increases, in this way a budget surplus would be much more probable and everybody would be happy. Under these circumstances, a further tax directly on corporate earnings might be avoided, thus making more certain for employees some further participation in national income with greater assurance of its stability when obtained.

It was Cardinal Richelieu, I believe, who told King Louis XIII of France that the purpose of any tax measure was to get the most feathers with the least squawk. I think I have improved on the Cardinal by actually growing more feathers. I have tried to remember my arithmetic which tells me that a lesser percent of more is oftentimes greater than a larger percent of less. And I am not unmindful of the reasonableness as applied to individual stockholders of the old saying in reverse, that is to say, if there is nothing to gain there will be nothing risked.

All people, including the economists of our Commerce Department, admit that more risk capital is necessary and the problem of raising it is important. I think if we are realistic about it, we can make two and two add up to four rather than to three as at present. In consequence, we should be able to see continued expansion and activity ahead.

INTRODUCTION

TO X

In the spring of 1949 an anonymous letter was dropped on the floor of the House of Representatives in Washington. It was dropped where it was bound to be seen and picked up. It charged that I, Floyd Odlum, had underwritten the cost of the last Truman campaign for President in return for a promise of huge orders to go to Convair (of which I was the executive head) for B-36 intercontinental bombers. Louis Johnson, Secretary of Defense, and Stuart Symington, Secretary of Air, were named as part of the conspiracy.

There was a drive at the time by the Navy for appropriations for super aircraft carriers. Symington and Johnson promptly recognized that this anonymous letter was a part of this drive, the purpose being, through charge of scandal, to set off a Congressional hearing which would bring the super carrier again to Congressional and public attention.

Within a few days the typing of the anonymous letter was traced to a typewriter in an important Navy office.

Finally, in August 1949, I was permitted to testify before the investigating Congressional Committee. My statement made under oath accompanies this preface.

The author of the letter was identified and on the stand admitted the falsity of the charges. The "conspirators" were cleared and complimented by the Committee. The Navy got its super carrier.

X

~~~~~~~~~~~~~~~~~~~~~~~~~~

During my more than thirty years of business life I have never once either asked for or received a business favor from any public official, although during that period I have had many friends and acquaintances in public office. The broad statement just made of course embraces a clear specific denial that I, either as an officer of Convair or otherwise, have asked for or that either Convair or myself has received any favor from Secretary of Defense Johnson, Secretary of Air Symington, or any other official in connection with procurement of the B-36 or any other procurement.

There is not one rivet of politics in the B-36; there is not one ounce of special favoritism in its more than three hundred thousand pounds of loaded weight. The innuendoes and insinuations concerning the B-36 order that caused this investigation by your Committee are completely baseless.

Convair is in the business of designing and building airplanes for both the Air Force and the Navy. It builds for them what they order and it strives to merit their continuing business. The Air Force has or will satisfy you on the point that the B-36 is the best plane available for the types of service to be done by it. That being the fact it is not only right that our Air Force should have an adequate quantity of the best but also altogether right that Convair, the designer of the B-36 and the producer of the original quantity, should also produce the additional seventy-five recently ordered.

Now I would like to present some pertinent facts.

I

Rumors which have been repeated on the floor of the House of Representatives carry with them the implications that Convair has had an unusual and unjustifiable share of the orders that have been given for aircraft by the Air Force. The contrary is the fact. Convair has fared less favorably than all the other major West Coast aircraft manufacturers in relation to increase in its backlog of orders since November 1947, which is when I became Convair's chairman. Convair's employees have substantially decreased during this period. If all of the present aircraft companies were to share in today's total aircraft business in the same proportion among themselves that they did during the War, Convair would be entitled to more orders than it has rather than less. The company that suffered the greatest cancellation of orders when seventy-five more B-36's were ordered from Convair has, even after such cancellations, the greatest backlog of orders on its books of any of the companies. Furthermore, at the same time that Convair received the recent orders for seventy-five more B-36's, Convair had approximately eighty million dollars of other production orders cancelled by the Air Force.

If this spells favoritism I hereby assign all Convair's rights to such treatment to its competitors.

II

The B-36 work has been anything but profitable. The entire fee earned to date by Convair on work on the B-36's, even before deduction of taxes, amounts to less than interest at the rate of 3 percent on the money that Convair has had invested in inventories specifically for the B-36 work.

Atlas Corporation has only approximately 6 percent of its assets invested in Convair. More than thirty-five thousand people either as Atlas Corporation or Convair stockholders have an investment in Convair and through that investment an interest in its profits. If there were no taxes on fees earned by Convair and all such fees could be counted as profits and could be paid out in dividends by Convair and then in turn by Atlas with respect to its 18 percent portion, I would, even before deduction of my income tax thereon, get less than $10,000 on all the profits that Convair has earned on all Government business since the beginning of 1946 to the end of 1948. My own income tax would take most of this back to the Government. Furthermore, Convair has had no profits during this period and it has paid no dividends since I have been even indirectly a stockholder.

When I became chairman of Convair I found that company in default under the terms of its credit agreement with a group of banks and on the verge of financial inability to carry on. It had been necessary for the company to borrow huge sums (approximately eight million dollars) to carry on the B-36 work alone. To make Convair solvent and able to carry on with its operations, Atlas Corporation bought more new Convair stock, much more than doubling its stock interest in Convair this way. It also, as an emergency measure to correct Convair's acute financial situation, while the new stock was in process of being issued, loaned Convair $7,000,000. This is what Atlas did for this aircraft company to make it possible to carry on economically and efficiently in building the justly famous B-36 and other outstanding aircraft. To date Atlas has received neither interest, dividends nor capital profits with respect to its Convair investment.

III

The uninformed might infer from the rumors not only that the B-36 carries with it large profits—the opposite of which has just been stated—but also that the B-36 work is something new for Convair—something that came about after I became chairman of Convair in late 1947. This second inference, like the first, is also contrary to the facts. As has already been brought out in the testimony, the basic requirements for this B-36 plane of a range of 10,000 miles with a bomb load of 10,000 pounds were established as long ago as 1941 to guard against the possibility of having to defend ourselves without the benefit of any bases abroad; basic design bids for this long-range bomber were then sought by the Air Force from aircraft companies, and as a result of competition by several aircraft companies Convair was awarded a contract in 1941 for two experimental B-36's; and a production order for one hundred planes was awarded Convair in 1943. Extensive flight tests starting in the spring of 1948 proved the merits of the plane beyond commitments or expectations, so that recently the Air Force ordered an additional quantity of seventy-five. The fact that these planes were ordered on the basis of merit and that the alternative would have been to buy a poorer product at greater cost seems not to have been considered or mentioned by those who gave rise to the scurrilous innuendoes.

While the B-36 was started back in 1941 the design has not remained static during these years. At least six major new versions have been developed to increase immensely the original performance, so that the B-36 has proven itself to the Air Force still to be pre-eminent, not only for long-range bombing but for long-range reconnaissance as well. In consequence the new order included reconnaissance planes as well as bombers.

Convair is active and will continue to be active in the development of further improvements for the B-36 which will again substantially increase the performance. Fortunately for the country in terms of economy the basic configuration of the plane is such that this increased performance can be achieved without starting all over again with a new basic design and all the time and expense in engineering, tooling, testing, reworking and the like that this would involve.

Few realize the time lost in developing a new plane. It can be readily seen that the B-36 is the product of several years' effort. Every plane in regular smooth operation is similarly the result of years of effort. There are undoubtedly planes on the drawing boards that will in time supersede the B-36 but this will be several years in the future. The point perhaps can best be brought out by the statement that no plane that reached the drawing board stage after Pearl Harbor ever shot down an enemy plane or bombed enemy territory during the last war.

IV

In addition to receiving from the B-36 the best performance for the tasks to be done by this type of plane, the people—that is to say, the taxpayers—are saved many millions of dollars by ordering seventy-five more of this particular plane rather than seventy-five of some new "just as good" model plane even if there had been a "just as good" one available, which there wasn't. Due to efficiency that develops in almost all manufacturing operations over the course of a particular job, each of the additional seventy-five new improved B-36's can be built for less than two thirds the cost of each plane of the original production order, all of which savings go to the benefit of the taxpayer.

The effect of this efficiency developed in the course of a particular production job is also such that much time is saved. This saving in time in the production of seventy-five more B-36's as compared with the production of seventy-five of a new type similar plane would be the equivalent of about nine months' operation of the whole Fort Worth plant of Convair employing fourteen thousand people.

V

Those who allege or insinuate that I paid "huge sums" into the Democratic treasury to get a large personal profit from an order for Convair for seventy-five additional B-36 planes have a weird and warped understanding of mathematics in view of what I said above. Now what are the facts about my contributions to the Democratic party treasury?

I contributed less than $5,000 to the Democratic campaign last fall; and I have contributed about the same amount to every

84

Democratic national Presidential campaign during the past twenty years. It is not wrong to be a contributing Democrat—it's not even bad manners. Furthermore, there is no inconsistency between being at one and the same time both a businessman and a Democrat.

VI

So much for my "huge" contributions. Now about my association and friendship with the Secretary of Defense and the Secretary of Air.

Secretary of Defense Louis Johnson is a friend of mine. It is my regret that I did not know him until I joined the Board of Directors of Convair in November 1947 where his own services as a director dated back to 1942. The country's gain when Mr. Johnson was appointed to the high post of Secretary of Defense was Convair's and my distinct loss. Since his appointment to this office I have not discussed Convair affairs with him at all and have seen him seldom.

As for my acquaintanceship with Secretary of Air Symington, with the one exception of a short social meeting several years ago, I met him for the first time in July 1948, which incidentally was after he had publicly proclaimed the outstanding merits of the B-36. Secretary Symington has as one of his major duties the problem of keeping our aircraft industry alive and alert. It would be impossible for him to perform his duties without meeting repeatedly with executives of the various aircraft companies. He probably knows several of them better than he knows me, although I hope not more favorably. I have talked with Secretary Symington on a few occasions about Convair and about the B-36, but always on his own initiative. Usually, my talks with him have been about the more general problems relating to air power.

By what I have said above I do not wish to minimize my sincere friendship for Stuart Symington. His outstanding and intelligent battle for air power brought his abilities and forthright character to my attention even before I knew him personally.

85

I pledge my continued support to Secretary of Defense Johnson and Secretary of Air Symington in the work they are doing. I never have and never expect to ask any business favor of them or anyone else in public office, but on the other hand it is only right and fair that neither I nor Convair shall be penalized now or in the future because someone chooses to float baseless rumors and insinuations.

It is not strange or any innovation that men in business and government know each other. All of you in Congress have friends, acquaintances and past associates in the business world and, I dare say, you even now see them occasionally and when you do you still treat them as friends. The question is not whether one is rich or poor in friends and associations but whether friendships and associations are abused. They haven't been to the slightest degree in this case and I resent deeply any insinuation to the contrary.

Secretary Symington has explained to you his single visit to my ranch to see me. Because of arthritis I maintain my active business office during the winter months on my desert ranch. There during the winter I have many business appointments daily. I have been deeply interested in many ways in the aviation industry and in air power generally for the past twenty years and have been in many of the developmental activities that have resulted in our American aviation industry as we see it today. Aviation, besides being an executive responsibility for me, is also my hobby. It would be strange if I didn't have many friends from all over the world in all branches of aviation including Navy and Air Force who came to my office or my home both on business and as social guests. These include many aircraft and airline executives and pilots as well as officers in the Armed Services.

VII

It has been said that the most important question is whether I knew when Atlas bought a stock interest in Convair that there would be a reorder of B-36's. The answer is definitely *no*. When

Atlas bought an interest in Convair in 1947, no special thought was given to the B-36 except that it was a certain amount of military work on hand which would keep part of the company's facilities busy for a certain length of time. I had no thought that the B-36 might or might not be reordered until after it made successful flight tests in the spring and early summer of 1948. Naturally I was pleased when the additional order was received. But on the other hand I was not too disappointed when it was indicated in the early summer of 1948 that Convair at the conclusion of the order then on hand should rearrange its Fort Worth plant and start building the Northrop B-49. This proposed action had some satisfying aspects in that it would assure a high employment level at Fort Worth for a long time to come and also because I am a personal and long-standing friend and admirer of Mr. Jack Northrop, the designer of the B-49. I helped finance his company at its inception.

What I wish to emphasize is that the Fort Worth plant was likely to be kept active on one kind of plane or another. That plant owned by the Government and operated by Convair since the plant was built is recognized as one of the finest in the world in which to produce large planes. It is reasonable to assume that if we are going to have an Air Force at all, such a plant, owned as it is, will not be left idle.

And dealing with Convair's production ability, Convair built more heavy bombers during the war than any other company. The Air Force's famous B-24 as well as the Navy's Catalina Flying Boat were Convair products. Convair has designed and built more than fifty different types of planes.

I further state with pride that Convair met 100 percent the Air Force's highly important "Gem" schedule of production during 1948.

VIII

There is no truth in the rumor reported on the floor of the House that I have tried to combine several aircraft companies into a "super aircraft combine" or a so-called General Motors of the Air.

I have never discussed with Secretary Symington directly or indirectly at any time or place his possible retirement and relationship in any way with any aircraft company or companies or any other project or company whatsoever.

IX

Convair not only has not received more than its proper share of orders but Convair has received far less than the amount of work for its San Diego plant that Convair and said San Diego area might reasonably expect in view of the heavy falling off of employment in that area due to reduction in size of the Naval Base there. When employment by any branch of the Armed Services is reduced in a community like San Diego by from ten to fifteen thousand people, it is cause for public concern and corrective action if possible. Convair's San Diego plant at the same time is down to about 25 percent capacity and is employing less than half the number it did a year ago. I have mentioned that when Convair received the contract for some more B-36's it had other contracts and subcontracts cancelled. Some of these cancellations for work to be done immediately affected the San Diego plant employment severely. The order for the additional B-36's did not increase the present employment at Fort Worth although it did, of course, provide for the continuation of the level of employment at Fort Worth for a longer period of time.

X

What I most regret about the gossip that has been brought to the attention of Congress and the nation is that such unjustified "smear" attacks on public officials make it increasingly difficult to secure able, experienced men for government officers.

INTRODUCTION

TO XI

The accompanying address, "Danger Marks," was delivered in Los Angeles in April 1950 and was made on behalf of the National Conference of Christians and Jews.

I have never had any racial prejudice or religious bias. While I am proud that I am primarily of Irish ancestry, I recognize as well the strength of other racial stocks. Most of the great religions of the world have the same basic precepts. And any religion that looks forward and upward for guidance is much better than no religion.

XI

~~~~~~~~~~~~~~~~~~~~

Ex-Secretary of the Navy, John L. Sullivan, wrote me last fall requesting that I make a speech on behalf of the National Conference of Christians and Jews. His letterhead bore on it the following purpose of the organization: *"To promote justice, amity, understanding and cooperation among Protestants, Catholics and Jews, and to analyze, moderate and finally eliminate intergroup prejudices which disfigure and distort religious, business, social and political relations, with a view to the establishment of a social order in which the religious ideals of brotherhood and justice shall become the standards of human relationships."*

That bylaw sold me immediately. I told Mr. Sullivan I would go anywhere my arthritic bones would permit and speak before any group, whether in high school, on street corner or in banquet hall. I am glad he chose Los Angeles, for while I earn my bread and butter in the East, my home, my voting residence, is in the desert section of Riverside County, California. I am also glad that a Kiwanis Club luncheon proved to be the forum because I have great respect for your organization and the effectiveness of its members to analyze what is good for our communities and hence our nation, and then to translate into action a sound position.

When asked the other day for a title for my talk I spontaneously gave it as "Danger Marks," for I had been thinking about how things are going today in the world and I am disturbed because of serious basic danger marks I see. These basics are all directly contrary to the established objectives of Brotherhood Week and the purposes of the National Conference of Christians and Jews.

We are in the middle of a war today. We not only are fighting a war at this very moment but it is probably the most serious war we have ever faced. Our way of life, which we here in the United States find generally to our liking, is in peril, great peril—yes, even existence itself for a great many of us is at stake.

Shortly after V-J Day, Stalin published a new edition of Communist dogma titled *Problems of Leninism* and it said among other things: "It is inconceivable that the Soviet Republic should continue for a long period of time side by side with imperialistic states. Ultimately one or the other must conquer. Meanwhile a number of terrible clashes between the Soviet Republic and the bourgeois states will be inevitable."

In contrast with the above, I read a few days ago in a Los Angeles newspaper an interview with a returned American visitor from Russia, who said, "They [the Russians] say that capitalist and Communist countries can live in peace without necessarily even doing business with one another."

The first statement is direct from the horse's mouth, so to speak. The other could come from the same animal by a more circuitous and indirect route, whether the person knew it or not. It is representative in any event of one of the techniques of the Russian plan of conquest.

At about the time Stalin uttered the threat and forecast just quoted, he and his small group dominated approximately two hundred million people. Today they dominate nearer seven hundred million people. And they are ever on the move for more workers in their ideological quarries.

The United States of America is the mortal enemy of the system that Stalin and his small group of co-dictators would impose on the world. Our way of life must perish or theirs must, according to their own affirmations, and I believe them. They are utilizing everything in and out of the books to accomplish our downfall.

What is going on is rather lightly called by some a "cold war." Strike out the word "cold." It is coldly planned, true enough, but it is plain unadulterated war to destruction. While keeping an iron ring around themselves so that their "workers" may not know the truth, the boss dictators are fighting with everything they have in this, the Third World War. They shoot when they please. The Fourth World War, with its outright physical destruction in terrible form, will in my opinion assuredly come by attack on us unless we win and win fairly promptly the Third World War now on. The arsenal for the Communists in this, the Third World War, consists of deceit, propaganda, stirring up prejudice between race and race and group and group, and forcing us in defensive measures to extend ourselves economically to the breaking point, and if possible in ways that will be wasteful. Stalin and his associates hope to lead us into depression so that out of the dissatisfaction, unrest and turmoil that would ensue, and which they are now engendering with every means at their command, they may capitalize from within our own ranks, using our own people to conflict with others of our own by revolutionary process and thus save the risks to the Communists of an atomic or hydrogen bomb, guided missile type of shooting, searing warfare.

But they are getting ready for that type of attack too and hope to name the day for its surprise start as the Japanese did at Pearl Harbor. But Pearl Harbor will be peanuts compared to the next surprise strike from Russia unless we nullify it now.

Russia has a land army greater than the combined armies of the United States and all its allies or potential allies. Russia has the world's largest submarine fleet and is building more and more. Russia has an air force that already has strength in nearly all categories larger than our own, and is building more planes at a faster rate than we are. Russia, with the help of the plant and personnel that were taken over in Germany, has the atomic bomb and is well advanced in the field of guided missiles. You don't need to take my word for this. I am quoting on this subject the public statement made in San Francisco last week by Secretary of Air Stuart Symington.

I say all these things because I want to arouse you to our real imminent peril. The people in a democracy control our national actions in the last analysis. That means you. It is therefore not good for the people to fail to comprehend the danger marks about them. Democracy can only live on truth. Dictatorship of the kind we have in Russia has the initiative but can only live behind iron curtains and on lies. We are spending a large portion of our national income for defense—about fifty percent of our taxes goes that way. It should be spent as wisely as it is energetically. You should know about this and make your views known to others. Wastage should be a crime. Failure to spend where it counts most in the war of today and tomorrow rather than along the lines of a Normandy or an Iwo Jima, for pure example, should be a double crime. Geography and shore lines no longer count. There is today a frontier only between ideologies. Our front-line trench is the truth—for ourselves and as an offensive against our enemies. Truth must be known here. We should have an aggressive campaign of truth abroad. We should know as much about what goes on behind the Iron Curtain as we blithely publish about our own defensive plans. We should carry the message of our democratic ideology as aggressively and more so than it is being sabotaged today by Russian dictators.

If communism is our greatest danger mark, then next in line come home-grown prejudices and intolerances. I don't need to tell you that prejudices and intolerances are wrong—you know it. But they are positively dangerous as well. They are the stuff on which the germs of communism and chaos breed and grow. And they are being fostered by our enemies every second in the day without holiday or sick leave or featherbedding.

One cannot legislate a man's feelings. Man's inhumanity to man makes countless millions mourn. Consider what the prejudices of Hitler cost the world. And these inhumane attitudes come from

93

the heart and the mind. Understanding and respect for others must be learned. They are not natural traits. It is easy to contemplate tolerance benevolently after a good luncheon of today's sort, but later on I beg of you to think of this objectively and from the standpoint of our own national welfare as well as our own good and happiness as human beings living together in a society.

America is still the melting pot for humanity as well as the cradle of liberty. Here we have thrown together every race, color and creed—and out of the composite must come a harmonious whole. It's not strange that we have had our impacts of temperaments and races. Strains of every race and strands of every national make up the warp and woof of our American tapestry. An Irishman does not think or act like a Scotchman; or a Pole like an Italian. And in some cases we are hardly a generation away from the motherland, the old customs, legends and traditions.

The result is the so-called minority groups with their pressures. Oliver Wendell Holmes said, "If a man is a minority of one we lock him up." But the minorities we are talking about are not that kind.

You and I are parts of some minority or other. That goes for every race and every creed in this country. There is nothing inherently wrong about being a part of a minority—a view that some of my Republican friends will gladly support. So long as the minorities are trying to live together within the fabric of our chosen pattern of government and society, they have a right to be tolerantly and judicially heard. When they are banded together to destroy our Government they must be rooted out and destroyed. It's no longer a private fight. We should all get into it—all the other minorities.

We sometimes resent these minority pressure groups. We should in some cases rightfully blame these minorities who have seized upon civil rights and made them a club for political purposes and by so doing have not only obscured issues but postponed good results.

But please remember that here in the conglomerate of American life the minorities, taken together, make up the majority. And the rights of the majority so defined are paramount.

Al Smith in 1942 said, "The thing we have to fear in this country is the influence of the organized minorities because somehow or other the great majority does not seem to organize. They seem to think they are going to be effective because of their known strength, but they give no expression to it."

Every problem in the field of group relations is really a problem of individual relations to be individually solved. The germ of intolerance is pretty difficult for one to identify within oneself. But this can be done. If allowed to run its course, intolerance can be more destructive than most other diseases combined, for it is a psychological disease. Get your feelings toward your fellow man out in the open for analysis. If we want our rights respected we must see that the rights of others who are living within the framework of our society are respected.

If we in America, against our background of free institutions and economic well being, fail to work out proper patterns of human relations, democracy is indeed lost. Man can in this way be proved incapable of governing himself from within. The victories wrung out of two wars in our lifetime will prove fruitless unless we translate into reality the ideals of equality and freedom that belong with the word "America."

The cost of discrimination and intolerance in industry and commerce alone in terms of national income is tremendous, some say as much as thirty billion dollars a year. Discrimination makes for unhappiness, inefficiency and lower productivity.

Human dignity and vision are intangibles of industry. In factory or business, no one who does not respect the integrity of himself and those about him can be an asset to his company. No one who is hurt, angry or disillusioned is going to develop much in the way of ambition or vision. And we need these qualities and work of the right sort as never before. Businessmen cannot afford the wastage of intolerance and discrimination in their organizations. They must start to eradicate it in the front office.

The individual is most important to our society. The rights of a minority are the responsibility of all the people of the United States. That responsibility can be neglected only at your peril.

Happily brought up in a Methodist parsonage as I was, and moving about with my preacher father from town to town, and meeting in these new places communities of Swedes or Poles or English, I never knew what intolerance was. I see good and bad in all as individuals but not as groups or races. I wish we were all that way.

America has its resources, open spaces, opportunity and freedoms. Let us preserve it for ourselves and our posterity—all of us. Let us do so by treating our fellow Americans as brothers, as a part of one great majority supporting our system and way of life, made up of individual human beings entitled within this framework to their little differences and personal opinions, even as you and I.

Because of the danger marks all around us and the forces trying to engulf us, it is time for us all again, for our mutual benefit, in the language found at the end of our Declaration of Independence, to "mutually pledge to each other our lives, our fortunes and our sacred honor."

INTRODUCTION

to XII

The first plant constructed in the United States solely for the purpose of making guided missiles was built at Pomona, California. It was built and operated by Convair for the Navy and produced the "Terrier," a comparatively short-range missile. There was quite a ceremony at the laying of the cornerstone on August 6, 1951, and I, as head of Convair, turned over the first shovelful of dirt and made the speech, followed by one on behalf of the Navy. My speech on that occasion accompanies this preface.

We are hearing much today about the "Atlas" intercontinental ballistic missile. I am proud to say that it was originally designed by Convair back in the late "forties" with funds provided for the purpose by our Air Force. The day I presented to the Directors of Convair a small-scale model of this three-stage missile is deeply etched in my memory. Also I take pride in stating that when government funds were no longer forthcoming for this project, the Directors of Convair on my recommendation appropriated Company funds to keep the development work going. In this way, when later public funds for the "Atlas" were again appropriated, precious time had been saved.

XII

~~~~~~~~~~~~~~~~~~~~~~

The Wright brothers, in their first powered flight, went about the length of our present-day B-36 bomber. At the time it was a fantastic feat and in retrospect it was a world-shaking achievement. Many more almost incredible advances have followed since then in our conquest of the air. Many more will take place in the future because, as Edwin Markham said in his poem titled "To the Top of the World": "Every goal is . . . only a camp for the night in man's eternal flight." He added prophetically about man—because his words were written in 1926—"Yes, sometime he will pass the earthly bars, laugh and reach out his hand among the stars."

We are participating today in another important historic event in the field of aviation—the start of the first large plant to be devoted entirely to the mass production of guided missiles. We are truly starting to reach for the stars.

In order to continue to live as free people—grownups who can bask in the noonday sun of security and contentment and children who can playfully and happily look forward to the future—we must keep absolute control of the air above us and the approaches to our shores.

A substantial portion of that most important task is on the broad shoulders of our efficient and ever alert Navy. It is our Navy which is building this guided missile plant. I, as chairman of Convair, on behalf of all my fellow officers and employees, say that we are filled with pride and with deep thanks that Convair has been chosen by the Navy to supervise the building of this Pomona plant and thereafter to operate it. We have worked hard to be among the foremost in this new field of electronics and guided missiles—which even now in its full scope lies mostly beyond the horizon—in order to justify this mass production job on which we are now embarked. As agents and servants of the Navy we pledge our best to justify their faith in us.

While we are today doing the seemingly impossible and accomplishing an incredible advance, in sending into the upper atmosphere and beyond, flying weapons which intelligently act without human pilots, we—all of us—must nevertheless still keep our feet also firmly planted in current production of conventional aircraft. This is a transition period we are in, one of indefinite duration, and too much must not be expected too soon in the way of these futuristic weapons. This is no time to let down our guard. The "Terrier" which will be built at the start in this Pomona plant is properly named. But I forecast that, before much time has elapsed, it will be as obsolete as the dodo bird and that other and better missiles will be coming off this production line. I hope so, for that means progress. And when better guided missiles are being produced here for the Navy, Convair hopes and expects to have developed them under Navy orders and as the Navy's agent to produce them.

To the people of Pomona, we say we will outdo ourselves to be good neighbors and to make Convair an efficient public servant in this area as elsewhere.

This is a great America, of which we have the good fortune to be a living part. It belongs neither to the dictators on the one hand nor to the socialists or communists on the other. It belongs to us—the people—and as a democracy it is ours to make or break. By ours, I mean all of us.

INTRODUCTION

TO XIII

The accompanying speech, which I made in October 1951 at San Diego before the National Securities Traders Association, speaks for itself.

To a degree, it repeats what I have said in other speeches in this bound volume, but some things bear repetition.

XIII

~~~~~~~~~~~~~~~~~~~~

Sometimes I think I must be approaching maturity. The rumor is false that I was a bugler in the Civil War. However, my organization did build and operate for the Government a munitions plant during World War I (incidentally without profit). I did serve on the War Board during World War II. And now World War III finds me at the chairman's post in the management of one of our greatest aircraft companies, Convair, with its headquarters and one of its principal divisions right here in San Diego.

This business career, extending over nearly forty years, has placed me in many vantage points and observation towers and has given me fair opportunity to view the merry-go-round of American business and politics. It is with that background that I approach the subject you have given me for this evening's talk, "Free Enterprise and What We Are Doing to Preserve It."

The university I attended was located in the wide-open spaces of Colorado at the foot of the snow-covered Arapaho peaks. The atmosphere there was one of freedom and of opportunity. It is little wonder that I started out as an individualist, a firm believer in states' rights and an early supporter of the doctrine of laissez faire, which in effect means it is best for the Federal Government to leave business alone. In those days one could slaughter for the market one's own chickens in one's own back yard via the time-honored head and hatchet method, without considering the implications of the Interstate Commerce Act. One could also write to a friend casually about an investment or even a speculation without wondering whether the letter could be considered "an offering" requiring a prospectus, forms, applications and hearings.

How different must be the viewpoint of people of younger years who nowadays come into a world of different hue and leave school to make their living by treading their way through a mystic maze of Federal laws and regulations too numerous for anyone to know about and too confusing for even the United States Supreme Court to define except by the usual split decision.

In those days when I started out to earn my living, the national income was only about one eighth of what it is today, the effective Federal income tax rate was about 1 percent and the total cost of combined Federal, state and local government was less than 8 percent of national income.

Times have changed. Today the cost of government alone, entirely apart from defense expenditures by the Armed Services, is running at the rate of well over 16 percent of national income. Today the man in the highest income brackets, which reach 91%, pays so close to all he earns that he can never catch up with himself again out of income if he makes a substantial mistake in any one year's computation of taxes due.

What has brought about these changes in our national life? From 1918 to 1931, I spent a great deal of my time in many foreign countries, acquiring and reorganizing businesses and dealing with public authorities. In these countries during this period I came face to face with bureaucracy. To me bureaucracy came to mean masses of people on the public payroll who were obliging enough to work on the so-called governmental aspects of any project but who seemed to be working more for the sake of activity than to get things done. For to get things done quickly would not only require exercise of responsibility but would also make fewer bureaucrats necessary.

And during those years each time I came home for a spell of work I found the movement toward bureaucratic form of government growing rapidly in our own country. I wondered if we were just growing up as a nation and in doing so were adopting the methods of the older, more matured nations. I saw interest rates go down generally, but at the same time I saw venture capital and the venturesome spirit in business pretty well disappear. As I viewed the passing scene and considered how our railroads and our electric power companies and many other wonderful projects were built, I oftentimes bemoaned the passing of the so-called buccaneers of industry. I've known many a rugged individualist who made two industrial blades of grass grow where one grew before, with benefit for all, and who made an abundance for himself in the process, but I've never known one of them yet who took it with him when he passed on.

But if I should stop my remarks at this point, I would be clearly misunderstood.

I no longer believe in the doctrine of laissez faire. Our national life has become much more complex, state lines have become less important in the business and prosperity of our people as a whole, and states' rights have had to become subordinated to national interests. I don't view everything that the Federal Government does with a jaundiced, belligerent eye. In fact, some years ago I appeared in a Town Hall of the Air debate supporting the proposal that business and government could work together. The opposite side of the question was taken that night by Senator Taft.

And there is almost a greater closeness and interdependence today between all the peoples of the world than there was fifty years ago between the peoples of some of our own states. The airplane, the telephone, radio, television and the press have seen to this annihilation of space and contraction of time.

There has been a term coined to take the place of laissez faire which seems to represent more modern thinking. That term is "free enterprise," but like all other words and terms it needs defining before it can be discussed. Today even the Russians claim that they are democrats and we are imperialists. My answer to that, in the language of the poets, is that a rose by any other name smells just as sweet. What we have, no matter what called, is perfection compared with the Russian system.

Free enterprise does not mean that we the people are to get something for nothing. Nothing is "free" in that sense. It does mean, however, that the individual is important and that the state is the servant of the people, to look after their group needs such as defense and policing and the like. Under a free enterprise system, the individual must be free

(a) to choose the business or profession he desires,
(b) to manage his affairs with such governmental limitations, restrictions and interference as are necessary to protect basic public overriding interests and objectives,
(c) to enjoy the fruits of his successful efforts,
(d) to move from one section of the country to another or from one occupation to another.

For "free enterprise" to work as defined above, society must assure individuals of

(a) hope of reward,
(b) private ownership,
(c) sanctity of contracts,
(d) competition.

Do we have free enterprise today? Whether we have it in full or not, my definition of free enterprise, which is not by any means original, is just the opposite of what they have in Russia and the satellite countries.

I mentioned at the start of my remarks that we are in World War III. I refer to the so-called "Cold War." And for us the Russian Cold War attacks have to do with free enterprise and its preservation.

I believe that the Communists' strategy is about as follows: Under threat by them of an open, hot fighting war, we must rearm. If we do not rearm, they will surely strike to conquer with their planes, tanks and men. But the other horn of the dilemma is even more engaging from the Russian standpoint. If we do carry through that mighty effort to defend ourselves and strike back in the air and on the sea and land, we must spend prodigious sums. We must tax the people heavily and we must impose restrictions on prices, on wages, on spending and on profits. We can invite national bankruptcy by careless mass spending. Furthermore, by too many interferences with individual initiative and enterprise, by too much regimentation, by too much government in business, and too great a subordination of the interests of individuals to the interests of the state, we can end up with something not too distinguishable from what the comrades behind the Iron Curtain now have. We can in this way prevent the shooting war but once again lose the peace.

And so I say there is a dividing line between what the Government can do with us in an emergency and what they should do. If our public servants take onto themselves too many of our rights, we will no longer have democracy except in hollow form and we will no longer have free enterprise.

It is the task of all the people, whether grouped in what is called industry or not, to see that this march toward bureaucracy and control by politicians does not run amok under the guise or even the requirements of military preparedness or war. It is up to the voters to devote the necessary time to the study of national and international affairs to be able to vote intelligently and to recognize demagoguery whenever and wherever it appears. We want to maintain a democracy, not to create or support a "demogracy."

Where are the greatest danger points for us?

First of all the expenditures for defense by our public representatives must be carefully made according to a basic plan and a sound strategy, or there will be costly wastage. To treat the dollar something like confetti and to shovel it out for every type of armament and defense in every place at any time is as futile as the act of the man who simultaneously jumped on three horses and rode off in three different directions.

As rich as we are as a nation, we cannot stand triplicate or quadruplicate spending of this nature. If today we do have a clear all-over plan, then I believe large parts of our population, including many of our public officials, are confused as to what it is.

In the second place, as we spend more for the Armed Services, we must spend less, if humanly possible, for the routines of civil government. As our population grows larger and our national business becomes greater, it would seem that government should be run for a lesser percentage of the national income rather than the contrary. But the actual cost in terms of percentage of national income as well as in dollars seems to keep going the other way. If we find the overhead of a business, in relation to volume of business, increasing, even though the volume is constantly increasing, we can be pretty sure something is wrong. It would seem to be equally true in government. What I am saying is that we need more economy and more efficiency. While we must accept temporary controls of many sorts in periods such as the one we are going through, it would seem that the standard to work toward should be more business in government and less government in business.

The statement that the power to tax is the power to destroy is almost as old as it is true. Today, when considering free enterprise and its preservation, one must give attention to the tax measures almost above all others. I fear—indeed I firmly believe—that taxes are being imposed today in a way destructive of free enterprise, private initiative and the profit system. The effect of a particular tax provision on our social structure seems very often to be given more weight in the deliberations of our legislators than the ability of that tax provision to produce revenues.

Many of the higher bracket taxes have long since entered the zone of diminishing returns. Less than one tenth of 1 percent of the national income still remains untaken by taxes in brackets of income over $100,000 yearly. Only about 9 percent of the national income remains untaken by taxes in brackets above $8,000 per year. And yet we go on increasing taxes in the upper brackets as if the object of taxation were to destroy wealth and exclude profits from our lives.

We must nowadays have as heavy taxes from every source as can be imposed in a way consistent with the continuation of our American system and way of life. But taxes can be obtained only where money is. And money is almost entirely in the middle and lower brackets. Any increase of income tax that does not hit these groups will not raise more money, words to the contrary notwithstanding.

Let me use the example of Consolidated Vultee Aircraft Corporation as to how taxes are working. Convair, on its work for the Government, after the usual disallowances, receives a fee of approximately 4½ percent on cost. But under the tax law, it will have to pay about two thirds of that back to the United States Treasury, leaving for the stockholders about 1½ percent on cost of work done. An individual stockholder in the high tax brackets, on receipt of his portion of this 1½ percent as dividends, in turn will have to pay back more than 80 percent of it to the United States Treasury, leaving him as his own about one third of 1 percent.

I venture to say that new money for equity capital will dry up under these circumstances. You securities dealers know that there has been a trend in industry toward financing more and more with borrowed capital, because common stocks have been selling below true values, and primarily for the reason just stated.

But things are really worse than just stated, because in arriving at taxable income available for the stock, the corporation can only deduct for depreciation based on cost of plant and equipment, whereas the company will have to replace machinery and equipment and buildings at perhaps twice original cost. The true earnings, therefore, are really considerably smaller in many cases than reported earnings. These faults in our system of taxation will catch up with our industrial strength in time. A profit-less economy may work in a slave state, but it won't work in a world of free enterprise, which we should not give up through bungling of the efforts to preserve it.

For emphasis, let me use Convair again as an example. Even with an increasing volume of business next year that will strain to the limit the strength and endurance of personnel, there will for the entire year be left for stockholders, before they pay their own taxes on it, not more than $100 per employee. For this, these stockholders have risked about $50,000,000 of their own money and almost a like amount of borrowed money ahead of them. This I say is straining free enterprise to the limit.

The so-called capital profits tax is even more of a snare and a delusion than the income tax. It is not in the taxation systems of England and many of the other nations, and for good reason.

Our Constitution, by amendment, gave Congress the power to tax income but no power to make a capital levy.

In a period of inflation, where everything goes up in dollar value but not in barter value, a tax on a dollar profit on sale of a capital item is nothing short of a tax on capital. We did not have inflation when the system of taxing capital profits was instituted. We do have inflation now and I believe that before long our highest courts will be faced with the question of when a tax on theoretical but not real profits becomes a tax on capital. You traders know that when two customers with equally good investments, having a present value in excess of cost, trade them between each other, neither is better off intrinsically but each has had to pay a tax on the transaction.

Of all the things I have mentioned as destructive of our free enterprise system, probably inflation, long continued, is worst of all. If I were Stalin I would chortle with glee to see the disruption and destruction that is eating away at our roots through inflation.

Inflation, I believe, can be controlled but it takes firm intention and a strong hand. No restrictions are too severe that will prevent the further rise in costs and consequent falling value of the dollar, provided those restrictions do not, in and of themselves, change our system of free enterprise.

In fighting communism from without, we should also be on guard against home-grown prejudices and intolerances.

I might also add as one more danger mark in connection with the maintenance of free enterprise, the apparent willingness and even desire of many patriotic people to make public, on at least a piecemeal basis, our military secrets. This is playing directly into the hands of the enemy. I believe thoroughly in freedom of the press, but freedom of the press should not be confused with freedom of an individual possessing secret information to make it public property.

I have heard the following question raised repeatedly lately: How can an industrially backward nation like Russia, pitted against the might of the greatest industrial nation the world has ever seen, come up with an air force larger than our own and also with mighty tanks and submarines and other modern armaments? The answer, to me, is simple. They have not done this by throwing around rubles. The answer is in a four-letter word—"work."

Those who wish to keep our bountiful and contented way of living, those who wish to look confidently forward and upward rather than over their shoulders with dread, those who wish to trust and enjoy their neighbors rather than to fear them, should ponder over this word "work." I am not talking about scales of pay. I am not even talking about longer hours. I am not talking only about the worker in the factory. I am suggesting that, in these exceedingly critical times, everyone in every occupation and walk of life should put more effort and efficiency into the work he does during given hours at the task. This will bring results faster than the greatest appropriations that Congress can make.

Free enterprise is worth saving. There has been a slippage. Free enterprise and its handmaiden democracy are not just words in the dictionary. They are real things that have brought us to the living standard and the level of contentment we have today.

They are worth fighting for, both at home and abroad. One place to fight for them is in your daily lives, by educating your fellow men to the facts of political and business life, by insisting that qualified men represent us in government—men who not only understand economics and business and industry, labor and payrolls and social problems, but who also realize that they are not our masters but in fact our servants.

That is the job of industry, but no less the job of securities dealers. I wish that all our people could have the knowledge that you have of what is going on in the world, and the understanding of the implications, and the contacts to pass this understanding on to others.

INTRODUCTION

TO XIV

Only once have I made a political speech. That was on the eve of the 1952 national election and it was made over the radio serving my home area in Southern California. My wife, Jacqueline Cochran, had been one of the moving factors in getting General Eisenhower to run for President. She had declined the nomination of the Democrats in our Congressional district to run for the House of Representatives because of her belief in "Ike." I was also strongly for him, as the accompanying speech discloses.

XIV

~~~~~~~~~~~~~~~~~~~~

I am registered as an Independent voter. In 1932, and afterward, I voted for Roosevelt and then for Truman. This year I am voting the Eisenhower ticket.

I urge everyone to vote. The reason is simple. In our democracy the people rule, but only through their vote on Election Day. Those who fail to vote temporarily lose their right to have a voice in determining the kind of government they want. If enough fail to vote, the power passes to groups and cliques, and the result is no longer a truly representative democracy.

But it is not enough just to vote. The voter must give careful thought and judgment to his vote. Without this thought and judgment, a machine could vote as well. It is not enough to vote a certain way because a political boss, or a business boss, or any other kind of a boss tells you to. Voting this way is a surrender of personal rights. People also vote in the countries behind the Iron Curtain, but they all vote one way according to boss rule. It's wonderful that in this country secret voting is positively guaranteed. No one but the voter knows, or ever can know, what goes on in the voting booth.

As of last week about fifteen percent of the registered voters of this country were still undecided. That to me is a good sign. The people are thinking. That undecided vote will put either Eisenhower or Stevenson into office.

I am surprised by the number of people in the community who, in my opinion, have a wrong understanding of the real issues they must pass on tomorrow. That is why I am speaking tonight on my own initiative at my own expense. I do not ask you to vote my way. But I ask you to consider carefully what I am saying and then to exercise your own careful, honest judgment.

Last winter I concluded that, despite my long association with the Democratic party, and regardless of the effect on me personally, I would have to work for a change in our national administration. I realized that democracy was off-course, and concluded that General Eisenhower was the man most likely to put it back on the road. I studied his record, had correspondence with him to make sure of his views on important domestic questions and finally went to see him in Paris.

It was a bit startling in the early days of last winter for a supposed Democrat to come out publicly for Eisenhower. *Time* Magazine asked me for my reasons. I put them on paper. They seem as good to me now on further reflection as they did then, so I will read that statement.

I want Dwight Eisenhower as our next President because, in my opinion, among all the candidates, he can best give us inspiring leadership during a period when we will be needing badly both inspiration and leadership; because he well understands the menace from abroad and how best to mobilize efficiently and economically our national resources of men and matériel and our foreign friends to meet such menace; because I know he understands that, by a course of wasteful national spending accompanied by destructive taxes and a heavy overburden of bureaucracy, we will destroy the very way of American life that we are seeking to preserve; because I know he believes that human rights and property rights are an indivisible package, one part of which cannot be lost without losing all down the drain; because I know he believes that states' rights are being submerged in growing and overwhelming national assumption of powers and that there should be a tendency toward restoring the dignity and powers of the states in matters that can be handled as well or better by the states; because he has worked all his life with youth and therefore understands youth, who is our promise of tomorrow; and because while he will be the leader of a party and will act as such in party affairs, he has not been steeped in politics and therefore will be more likely to surround himself with a proper blend of advisers and administrators than will a dyed-in-the-wool politician.

I have not time to discuss all these points so I will deal only with a major underlying problem.

In my opinion, communism is the greatest threat the American people have ever faced. In our daily activity, with so many things seemingly going well, it's hard for many of us to believe this but it's true.

We in America are faced with two equally dangerous extremes. We can underarm, in which event a general war would be almost certain, with ourselves the loser. Or we can insure, by tremendous building up of armaments, that this won't happen. We need even more defense production. But if we spend wastefully on defense long enough, a depression will eventually develop with social unrest and all the other things the Communists want us to have. They are planning things that way.

We must find the sound balance point between these two extremes. We must not be underarmed, but in getting our armament we must not get so much of it too expensively. We must eliminate the waste and get more for the same money through better planning and consequent better use of our manpower and facilities.

My belief is that General Eisenhower is most qualified to keep us soundly balanced between these two extremes. He knows the military strength of the Communists and how to meet it. He is in position to judge as to what Americans and all allies can best put respectively into the common defense pool. He is best equipped to keep the other free Western world countries working with us, because he has already worked with them successfully. With a background of extremely fine service to the nation as a soldier, he has developed in his later years of work high-grade capacities in administration and diplomacy.

I do not know too much about Adlai Stevenson; and most of my listeners do not know much about him either. In making a choice, wishing to get the best out of the President's office, it seems to me we can count much more surely on a man who has worked constantly in this field of defense and diplomacy rather than on one who has a purely political background.

It's true that Eisenhower is not a professional politician—and I say thank God for that. It's not a professional politician we need. We need a man who is honest beyond doubt, clear-headed beyond doubt, and one who is not tied up with strings as to the past or deals as to the future.

That's why, among other reasons, I am for Eisenhower. To me politics is not a game to be played by politicians for their own benefit and enjoyment. We need real leadership today as we have never needed it before. We need statesmen and diplomats in our top national jobs—not professional politicians. It's very strange to me that President Truman tried to get Eisenhower to run on the Democratic ticket, and when Eisenhower could not be obtained as a Democrat went whistle-stopping against him.

A good man is good whether he is on the Democratic or Republican ticket. Patriotism, clearness of purpose, judgment, ability and leadership are not matters of party emblem but of personality. Eisenhower has all these qualities and most of us know he has them because Eisenhower has been passing before us in critical review for years.

And let us not take lightly the qualifications of the respective Vice Presidential candidates. Nixon is from our own state. His home is nearby. He is young, active, and his record is good. Sparkman, on the other hand, is apparently the kind of a man who runs—as he actually has—in the South on a ticket with a party label calling for white supremacy, while at the same time trying to make the Negroes of Harlem think that he and the Democratic party are the real champions of civil liberties. The Democratic party has its tap roots in the Deep South, and the Deep South has not been known as the champion of the rights of Negroes.

General Eisenhower may not have that same oratorical mastery of the smooth-flowing English sentence that Stevenson has. But wise-cracking and witty, well-delivered speeches are not the yard-stick by which to measure statesmanship and leadership and knowledge. I prefer rough-hewn solid words from the heart and from the depths of experience.

In this connection I noticed in Friday's paper what Ellen Stevenson, ex-wife of Governor Stevenson, had to say when stating that she would vote for Eisenhower. She said: "If words should become more important than deeds, democracy will find that the English sentence has become a sentence of death."

The Democrats are saying, "You never had it so good." Just whom are they referring to? Can it be the well over one hundred thousand boys who have been casualties in Korea or their relatives at home? Can they be referring to the housewife who finds that take-home pay has not been keeping up with the rising cost of the contents of the market baskets? I know the slogan is not true applied to me, whether as a California rancher or otherwise. It undoubtedly is true, however, as to President Truman himself.

Let's not be carried away with false slogans. Nothing is good for you in the long run that is not sound for your democracy. On the verge of a physical collapse a shot of dope could make you feel good. The Government's debt is your indirect debt which you must eventually help pay personally. Inflation and defense spending act as the dope that makes some of you feel temporarily good.

I have just come across a remarkable political poster. It says that it is the public who pays. It adds that the mounting national debt is terrible. It says that there must be a balanced budget and that our national leadership has brought us to the verge of bankruptcy. It pledges a 25 percent reduction in taxes and asks that the spendthrifts be turned out and responsible government be put in.

The remarkable thing about this poster is that it was issued by the Democratic National Campaign Committee in 1932 to elect Roosevelt and Garner.

The public debt then was about twenty billion dollars. It is several hundred billion dollars now. The annual deficits under the present administration have made the 1931 deficit look like chicken feed. There is a distinction between dollar bills and confetti which the present administration either disregards or does not recognize. Long experience has taught us who the spendthrifts really are and they are experts through long practice. I join with Jim Farley in his words of 1932 just quoted and which I now repeat: "Turn the spendthrifts out."

INTRODUCTION

to XV

The Wings Club of New York is an organization of aviation partici-
pants and enthusiasts, including pilots, manufacturers, designers, airline operators and writers.

Each year the Wings Club holds a big anniversary dinner. At their
November 1952 meeting I was the principal speaker. The speech follows.

XV

~~~~~~~~~~~~~~~~

Every person in this room tonight over fifty years of age was living before the first powered flight of the first airplane.

That is really an astounding statement, considering that today most of us travel by air, the aircraft industry is one of our largest employers, and our very life and freedom depend primarily and perhaps altogether on the pre-eminence of our air power.

The Wright brothers, when they made that flight at Kitty Hawk in 1903, probably did not realize that they were changing the course of world events, causing some empires to wane and other peoples to rise. My wife has on her trophy table a piece of the fabric from that first plane. I often look at it and wonder if we might not have been better off if the Wrights had rolled that flying machine back into the hangar before its first takeoff and and called it a major mistake in such a convincing way as to end all future flights.

Certainly we will face our destiny in the air. We, therefore, had better keep most alert to the man-made wings that for good or bad are about us in increasing numbers, lest we have nothing left for us to hear except the rustle of angels' wings.

I was never one for statistics. I think they have romantic appeal only at a convention of insurance actuaries or in a study by Kinsey. However, I cannot stand here on the eve of the second half century of aviation without counting a few of the marks in the onrush of the conquest of the air. The Wright brothers' plane, if it had taken off on that first flight down the length of one wing of a B-36 bomber, would have come to rest on the other wing substantially short of its tip. Now we are flying around the world nonstop. The Wright brothers' engine weighed many pounds per horsepower. Now the power plant weighs less than one fifth of a pound per horsepower or its equivalent in thrust. The first airplane rose only about ten feet from the ground. But now man has flown close to 80,000 feet above the earth's surface. The first plane had a speed of about thirty miles per hour. We now talk of speed in terms of mach, one mach being the speed of sound. It has been exceeded often and planes of mach 2 speed are already in the process of being built. These statements could almost be thought of as fantasy but they are cold facts and this progress merely points the way to the rush of the future.

Way back in the dim past, we are told, the progenitor of man —of course in different and much simpler form than the present biped called Homo sapiens—crawled out of the water into the slime and then out of the slime onto ground and learned eventually to live on land. Most of man's early relatives stayed behind and are looked down upon by us as "poor fish." Some others managed to shake both water and dust from their feet for short periods and are known as birds. These fish and birds developed their own radar and pressurized suits and weather forecasting, while man was apparently lagging behind—just dawdling around slowly on foot and developing his mind, particularly that portion of his mind that deals with logic and inductive reasoning, imagination, ambition and determination. So, after millions of years, man one day—just yesterday—decided that he would outdo the birds. Already we are making these birds look like landlubbers.

Whether we should have stopped trying to overcome gravity and space fifty years ago I have not the foresight to tell. But I know we cannot stop now. The flight of man into the upper air and beyond is truly endless, even if it proves to be like the flight of the moth into the flame and destruction.

Aviation has been more than a hobby for me and my wife, Jackie Cochran. I have been in many phases of aviation during the last twenty years. I have had manufacturers in my bedroom before sunup to get money to meet that day's payroll. I have helped bring into being prototypes of the backyard and hangar designed variety and have followed racing which has served greatly as a proving ground for aviation. I have been a director of engine companies and plane companies. At one time or another my company has been a major stockholder in most of our major aircraft companies. Indeed, seemingly to round out the picture, a plane crashed into my office through the side wall of my room on the 58th floor of the Bank of Manhattan building. This unfortunate visit was without appointment. My extracurricular activities include that of chairman of the Lovelace Foundation for Medical Education and Research out in Albuquerque. Medicine sounds quite distant from aviation but it isn't. The plane, in its technical advances, is leaving the pilot behind. More attention must be given to the human element. The Lovelace Foundation personnel, under Dr. Lovelace's most able direction, are doing research, among other things, in aviation medicine, and much is being learned and contributed to progress. Even more, under the auspices of our Foundation a book has just been published dealing with flight into the upper atmosphere and beyond. Serious people are thinking seriously about flight by man in the space out there where the atmosphere is left behind and the back side of the moon comes into view. The "wild blue yonder" is no longer a descriptive term. Things are being classified. The terms "air" and "atmosphere" are too general. We know now the "yonder" isn't even blue. Now we must talk about the troposphere, the stratosphere, the ionosphere, and other spheres or layers that must be traversed in the early part of flight before we reach space, which incidentally is reachable. We must be prepared to meet face-to-face the problems of boiling blood, planes burning from friction, and the challenge of star dust. I compliment and honor here and now the hardy first pioneers in flight who did not come back at all, or came back with early scattered bits of almost earthbound information. Whether any of you hardy souls here present ever reach the outer spaces of travel or not, no one can deny you the honor of being very instrumental in the conquest of the outer atmosphere, which conquest is just beyond our present horizon of knowledge.

And now I want to become exceedingly serious.

The Wright brothers had nothing they could permanently patent and control. While the first flight was in America, we have no monopoly on aviation or air power. We loosed on the world something that can turn on us and destroy us. And unless we change our national ways, we may be reckoning very soon with harsh destiny.

In World War II, when control of the air by piloted plane was taken away from the Germans, they came back nearly to win the air war with their pilotless missiles.

If we had been a few weeks slower with victory we might have been lost to Hitler dictatorship. Even so, we apparently have not learned our lesson.

Out of the ruins of Nazism, communism rose to challenge our way of life. Communism is the greatest threat that America has ever faced in all her history, and yet may not be recognized by many as such.

The over-all objectives and strategy of the Communists are well known and often announced. Why don't we take them to heart?

Last winter, after having been a supporter for a long period of the administration in power, I concluded that, regardless of personal consequences, I wanted to be counted among the ranks of those who thought it was time for a change—a change of whatever was necessary to bring about an awareness of the dangers and to put into effect policies and programs to deal adequately with these dangers. It was a conclusion founded on careful, prayerful thinking which caused much stomach tension. Fortunately, so many more felt the same way that my tension has been considerably released since Election Day.

Why did I feel this way so strongly? Because I had seen public officials who must have known better—at least, by application of the simplest logic to the bare facts should have known better—either ignore or disregard the strategic planning and movements of the enemy or, worse, fall into the trap. And I saw what I felt completely sure was underarming, when over-all strength is taken into account, but at a cost that should have given us adequate defensive and striking power. In other words, we were running at the same time into both the destructive extremes I have mentioned and it takes real experts in making political and policy mistakes to do that.

Now at the risk of sticking my personal neck out again, I am going to state some of the reasons why I have been of the opinion that we have been headed along the high road to catastrophe.

First and foremost, we have been told by our own people, who *should* know, that Russia has a stronger air force than we have. We are told that Russia has a greater number of planes and is building planes at a faster rate than we are. We are told that the quality of the Russian planes is good; that the Russians are comparatively deficient only in long-range striking power but are building that up now, not only in the field of bombers but also in the field of guided missiles; that at the same time they are building ever stronger and stronger home defenses against our own striking power. Consider the consequences of these statements if they are true. I doubt if there is anyone in civilian or military life who will take issue with the statement that air force will play a highly important role, even if not the supreme one, in either avoiding war or winning war if it comes. They may argue that the Navy or the Army or the Marines or all three should have their own air force in order to make our over-all operational striking power most effective. I am not directing my present statement to the soundness or unsoundness of any such point of view, which deals largely with the implementation of aircraft after they have been built and put into service. But I am talking about getting in the first instance, through planning and procurement and the like, the best, the quickest and the greatest dollar value of rounded air power achievable, whether the flight must be made from just back of the front lines, from carrier, or from bases way back home. In our private lives and through friendships, relatives in one branch of the service or the other, and for many other reasons, we can properly be Air Force fans or Navy fans, or Army fans, but as citizens, when we get down to rock bottom, we must all be for real unification of overall effort at the top with the coordination and the lack of duplication and the consequent overall greater strength at lesser cost that such efforts must bring. If, as the Good Book says, a house divided against itself cannot stand, then a house in which the foundation and the basic timbers are not well joined together will be comparatively weak. And regardless of what color you paint the timbers —Navy blue, Army khaki, Air Force blue, or Marine Corps green —it is inescapable that the joining agent must be the spikes of the new and great power born at Kitty Hawk forty-nine years ago.

It is this new and still growing power—the power to wrest decisive advantage from the air—that I emphasize here tonight. But if because I have accented the Air Force in discussing our future role in defense or offense, anyone here tonight at a meeting of airmen wishes to disagree and to put in a priority claim for the sea power or ground forces, I need only reply that we are again told that Russia has more land forces by far than ourselves and our allies combined. And we are also told that Russia is also far out ahead in the field of long-range submarines—the kind that can keep our troops and supplies from getting abroad by surface boats and that can launch guided missiles close to our shores.

Remember, furthermore, that size and quantity of our armament standing alone mean little. It is the comparative strength that counts and that is where we are told we are lacking.

Why are we in this alleged serious predicament? Is it because Russia has more steel capacity or aluminum production or other basic metals than ourselves? These are the things out of which planes, ships and guns are forged. The answer is "No" by a very

127

long way. Is it because she has more plant capacity or heavy equipment in factories or better railroad transportation than we have? The answer—at least when the Iron Curtain was rolled down—is again "No." Is it because she has more scientists or more skilled technicians or more experience and know-how than America and our allies? The answer is again "No." I worked in those behind-the-Iron-Curtain countries for many years between the two world wars and I know how backward most of them, including Russia, were industrially and how poor was their mechanical product. They were outstandingly weak in these ways during World War II when we had to sacrifice many hundreds of freighters and many thousands of lives getting our own war equipment to them. If in seven years Russia has moved from the bottom to the top in technique and capacity and available plant and production line power, then it is the strangest phenomenon in the history of the modern world. I say this even though, through the fullness of our democratic hearts, we stood by and let the Russians take German scientists, technicians and equipment back to Russia from East Germany.

The answer to this comparative Russian air strength and their faster momentum, if the allegations are true, must be found otherwise. It can be found partly on the Russian side but mostly in our own fair land. The Russians devote most of their comparatively small quantity of steel, aluminum and other raw materials to the making of planes, ships and guns, and most of their land transport to the carrying of same to and from factory. We devote most of our raw materials and transport to civilian uses that increase our standard of living. If we enjoyed a substantial margin of safety in our favor, then doing things this peace-loving and peace-expecting way would be well. But as my friend Senator Lyndon Johnson once said—"There hasn't yet been a television set designed to shoot down a Mig."

I feel sure the Russian worker is less adept and skillful than our American worker. But the Russian worker works longer and gives his full attention during the hours he is on the job to producing the greatest possible output. Again, while the Russian population as a whole is not much greater than our own (even excluding the population of our allies in industrial nations), a greater percentage of that Russian population is undoubtedly on the factory production line. There you have it from the Russian side.

Now what about here at home? Why are we not still pulling fast ahead of the rising Russian curve? One of the answers lies in the short four-letter word spelled w-o-r-k. We don't work as if our lives and our freedom depended on it, which they do to a greater degree than most people seem to realize. On our factory production lines we have become less efficient rather than more efficient. It takes more man hours to do the same thing than it previously did. Why should this be? I don't know. Maybe the workers have no conviction that their lesser output will really endanger themselves, their neighbors, and the safety and continuity of their way of life. Somehow they should be given understanding of this truth. This takes national leadership. Maybe these workers do not have a correct understanding of this problem because there is not true understanding among the labor leaders, on whom the workers rely for certain direction. I believe this lack of understanding of our critical situation among at least some of our more important labor leaders is probably true. If so, it is again the result of faulty national leadership.

I am completely convinced that we must start at the very top level in the task of tightening the belt and forging ahead. I refer primarily to the administration in Washington. We have as the starting point new and, I believe, exceedingly good top leadership. You can gather from this not only that "I like Ike" but also that I believe "Ike means might" founded on a knowledge of the danger we are facing and the realistic ways to meet it.

There is much needless duplication and waste in many ways, but mostly in the use of personnel. It runs into billions of man hours per year and the consequent dollar cost. Look at the national budget and you will see how very much of it goes for personnel in comparison to what goes for actual hardware.

We are one nation with one defense objective. Let's act as one in our planning and spending. We are not wealthy enough in men or materials to indulge in the luxury of waste.

We all hope that some day military organizations can be classified in a truly peaceful world as luxury forces. Unfortunately we have not achieved that period of history. As long as military forces are required, they can and must be acquired without waste. Much more than we have now must be created, but more dollars do not need to be spent and over-all taxes need not be higher and in fact could be less while getting greater results than we are now getting.

It's not enough to push upward the output of planes, ships, tanks and guns from present levels. In terms of effective defense forces and striking forces, our curve must be turned upward very sharply because the enemy, we are told, is producing at a heavy rate. And they had several years' start while we twiddled our fingers, so to speak. Even worse, we threw away the military organization and equipment we built up during World War II. We really did not seriously start building again until the Korean War. And in appraising what we need, remember that Russia has had and has the initiative and therefore can strike when and where she chooses. This initiative means much when it comes to appraising comparative strength. We need more of everything under these circumstances to hold our own.

If our knowledge of the Soviet activities and planning is even approximately correct, then our own planning is wrong. We cannot afford to get there slowest with the "leastest." But that seems to be what we are doing.

And if our facts about the Soviet planes, tanks, and ships and plans are wrong, that is the most tragic error of all. How can we hope economically and efficiently to plan and produce unless we know the problem to be met? Under these circumstances of lack of true facts we would be likely to try and get strong everywhere with everything. As a result we would forge a chain that would be weak in nearly every link. Facts are essential to any intelligent action. I believe we are spending far too little effort in this direction. Remember how lacking we were about German facts before the war and how expensive our negligence proved. Getting true facts at almost any cost is a way to save because it is the way to avoid ending up with expensive armaments which may be obsolete or useless.

At the start I spoke about the aircraft industry. That is a misnomer. It is not really an industry but a service. Practically everything made is for the government on pretty much of a straight fee basis. Adequate profit incentive to do better is lacking. This is not as it should be. The aircraft companies should not be required, through a wholly fixed price basis, to take the risk of inflation and consequent increases in labor and material costs, which are beyond the manufacturers' control and even beyond the ability to forecast in bidding for a long-term production contract. But aircraft companies should be entitled to get and keep, after taxes, a profit which includes a substantial variable constituting remuneration for increased efficiency.

Now I would like to discuss commercial planes. I believe that all the commercial transports that have been built by American aircraft companies since the end of World War II, taken in the aggregate, represent a net loss to such manufacturers. This does not make for a strong production industry. The aircraft companies should not be foolish enough to build at a loss. No airline should use the power of competition to force them to do so.

Let me say a word at this point about the presently much publicized British jet transports. Some of our United States airlines have been looking at them for possible purchase. I am not intending to criticize the United States airlines if they wish to buy British jet transports. The dollars these airlines receive from passengers, express and mail pay are not earmarked. If they must have jet transports before we can build them at home and such transports can be obtained abroad, that is that. But why cannot such jet transports be obtained in this country? It is certainly not because our American companies lack the ability to build them competitively with any producer in the world. There are two reasons. In the first place, plant and personnel are fully occupied at the present with work for the Armed Services. In the second place, our aircraft companies work mostly for the Government on a fee that leaves the companies, after taxes, only about two percent of sales, without taking into account stockholders' personal taxes. As a consequence such companies do not have the financial fat on their bones to lead off at the present time in such a venture which, unless many orders are received at one time, involves a very great financial risk which might in one fell swoop absorb profits for years to come.

These two reasons explain why the lead in jet transports rests in England at the moment and not at home. But it would be quite easy to reverse the situation. If American prestige abroad or American foreign trade is involved this is a matter of concern for our American Government. The action of the British Government makes it fairly evident that the British Government believes prestige and foreign trade are involved.

Given a release by the Government of the necessary manufacturing space, personnel and existing tooling, Convair, just as an example, could have a jet transport version of its B-60 ready by 1955. It would be a proven article because it would have built into it all the experience gained with the B-36 and the B-60. It would seat close to 200 passengers. It would cross the continent nonstop in less than five hours; and its seat mile operating cost would be very low. I am not engaged in sales promotion in making this statement. Other companies could probably do the same. I am merely pointing out why jet transports are not now being built by American manufacturers.

In connection with the building of our air power, I am constantly struck by the fact that the cost of aircraft is too high and should be reduced if humanly possible. I don't suggest I know the answer to this problem of cost of planes, but there must be an answer. It may be in new manufacturing methods. I think it is. It may be in the greater use of plastics rather than in the millions of rivets and other detailed work that make a plane maker's job almost as fine and delicate as a watchmaker's job. A cheaper plane does not have to last so long. And in any event the rush of aviation causes obsolescence to the usual metal plane long before the end of its physical life. A monument will be built to the man who finds a new way to build good planes with plastic, or otherwise much cheaper than planes are at present. He will need an experimental organization back of him and time. All that costs money. The Government does not provide much money for this kind of research work in new manufacturing methods. The aircraft companies, out of the small profits they have left after taxes, cannot presently afford to do more than skirt around the edges of the problem. They are, of course, doing such skirting. A piece of new metal shows up here and a piece of plastic there in connection with some specific production assignment, making for progress, although slow. What we need is revolutionary progress in this respect and that takes concentrated group effort and money not now available.

I would like to leave my talk on a higher note than war. It is pretty generally admitted that no one can really win the next peace through war. Apparently peace in the world cannot be gained that way. If there is constant clash now for living space, raw materials and markets, please remember that each year more people than the present population of Belgium and Holland combined are being added to the earth who must support themselves. These net increases of population will be cumulative. The pressures for even food and raw materials, let alone luxuries, will become greater and greater unless the way is found to make the earth more abundant and to take care of whole groups in the parts of the world now comparatively arid. Whoever contributes to finding this answer will rate more than a monument. If all people in all climates can be made reasonably healthy, with

even the less able and the less industrious having reasonable assurance of basic food and shelter, the clouds of international
trouble will in time give way to the sunshine of a more agree-
able world. I hope that our own generation who seem for the time
being, at least, to have lost their grip on peace, can reorient themselves and help find the new way and thus share the glory of
bringing about these peaceful objectives so devoutly to be
desired.

INTRODUCTION

TO XVI

While attending the University of Colorado Law School I specialized in mining law. In the early thirties I bought a vanadium mine for myself near Moab, Utah. It had in it so much of a useless mineral called uranium—which had to go onto the dump—that I sold the mine at a loss. Later, in World War II, when the uranium atom had been fissioned in chain reaction, that dump and others like it were bought up by the Government and the contained uranium went into the first atom bombs.

No wonder that when the uranium boom started with the biggest strike of all just five miles from my old mine, I became interested. And the more I studied the future uses of uranium, the more interested I became. The end result was Hidden Splendor Mining Company, the largest independent uranium mining company in America.

The uranium boom was a modern version of the gold rush and in the midst of it I had many rather fantastic experiences.

Uranium is slowly coming into its own. Within this decade the peaceful applications of nuclear energy will be manifold.

I made numerous speeches on the subject of uranium. I include in this collection one given in April 1955 before the Conference on Intermountain Industry in Salt Lake City.

XVI

〰〰〰〰〰〰〰〰〰〰

1.

Horace Greeley said, "Go west, young man," and Brigham Young, standing on the mountain heights overlooking the present location of Salt Lake City, said, "This is the place." I found their advice sound.

As a young man, I left the East, and I started to practice law in Salt Lake City. Forty years ago I was an assistant lawyer in the legal department of Utah Power and Light Company in an office on the fifth floor of the Kearns Building. I went back to that fifth floor last summer and looked over my old quarters. They looked good to me. I might say I was a trifle homesick.

The first law fee I ever earned was paid in a few thousand shares of a penny stock. My task was to draw the charter and bylaws for a copper company. Those shares proved worthless, but they still rest inside my lockbox as a memento. The first mine that I was ever interested in was a vanadium-uranium mine near Moab, Utah. That was about twenty years ago. We had to throw the uranium into the dump or tailings in those days. How times have changed!

This is like a homecoming day for me. Although I left Utah for New York in 1916, I have returned often, and while working in the East, I greatly prized a friendship I maintained with some of the leaders in the Mormon Church, including President Heber J. Grant and Bishop Nibley. It was my good fortune to start my business and professional career back in the teens with people of honesty and faith, among whom a man's word was as good as his written bond.

A fellow I have known quite well for a long time took up his pen years ago and wrote a rhyme about a certain spot in Utah on the Logan River which was known as "Hatch's Camp." That verse expresses my feelings, and I am going to take the liberty of reciting a part of it now.

When I'm tired and sick and weary
Of the din of city strife
And am longing for the pleasures
Of a natural open life,
Ship me westward to the mountains,
Put me off at "Hatch's Place"
By the Logan in the Wasatch;
There my sorrows I'll efface.
There before the open fireplace
Or stretched out beneath the trees,
I will listen to the music
Of the mountains and the breeze,
To the roaring of the waters,
To the song of melted snow,
Until night has brought its shadows
And the sky is all aglow.
And then the soothing kisses
Of a mountain air so sweet
Will comfort me until I lapse
Into a blissful sleep.

The author of those lines is here with us tonight. In fact, I'm that fellow. As poetry, it is a very feeble attempt. But as an emotional expression concerning a state I love, I stand by it. Hatch's Camp was owned by Hezekiah Eastman Hatch, one of the Mormon leaders of his day and father of Eastman Hatch who honored me with an introduction a few moments ago.

Eastman Hatch also suggested my subject for tonight: "New Treasure in the West." I assert that the real treasure in Utah is embedded in the hearts of her people, but Eastman definitely had uranium in mind, so I will get on with that subject.

The day before yesterday, Dr. Albert Einstein passed on. The atomic energy industry in due time should create a memorial to this great scientist. He was the one who led the way to the splitting of the atom and to the opening of the atomic era into which we are now embarked. Dr. Einstein stated in general effect that mass and energy are different forms of the same thing and that there is an accurate equivalence between the two. Indeed he gave the equation years ago. We are today converting some of the mass of the uranium atom into energy in conformity with that equation.

When a person burns a pound of coal, the gases and ashes left over seem on any ordinary test to weigh a full pound. In fact, however, an infinitesimal part of the weight of that coal has been converted into heat. In other words, some mass has been converted into energy.

When a pound of fissionable uranium atoms is fired up—that is to say, fissioned—through splitting of the atoms, three million times the amount of energy is released than in the case of the pound of coal. Therefore, for heat production, a pound of fissionable uranium is worth 1,500 tons of coal.

If the atoms in a sufficient-sized mass of fissionable uranium are split fast, a violent explosion results like the atomic bomb, accompanied by an immense amount of heat. If the same atoms are fissioned slowly, heat is produced but without the explosion. Such heat can be used in any of the many ways that heat from any source is usable.

We have learned both to split the uranium atom and to control the speed of the splitting or fissioning process. In other words we can prevent the explosion and regulate the heat. Therefore the peacetime uses of uranium are looming large right before us. It is of them I would speak tonight for they make uranium the new treasure of the West in general and of Utah in particular.

There are a few simple things we should all know about uranium. I will deal with them first. If they weren't fairly simple, I would not attempt an explanation because at best I am only a hillbilly, junior grade, in this field of discussion. My task has been to familiarize myself with the essentials that bear on the economics and the future of the uranium industry.

Have in mind first of all, please, that there are only 92 different kinds of atoms found in nature. All animal, vegetable and mineral things on earth are made up of combinations of one or more of these 92 atoms. Uranium is one of these 92 atoms— number 92 in fact.

An atom has never been seen because it is inconceivably small. If each of the atoms in a mass of atoms the size of a drop of water were in fact a drop of water, there would be enough water to keep Niagara Falls going at its present rate for about 2,000 years.

I now hold before you a cube which has three-way dimensions of between five and six inches. It represents the size of 140 pounds of natural uranium atoms. It is evident that uranium is heavy. It is in fact the heaviest of all the 92 elements. This is one reason why it is the important one in this modern alchemy of converting mass into energy. In other words, it has more mass represented by weight to convert.

But this cube of uranium as found in nature contains slightly different kinds of uranium atoms which are all chemically the same but which have slightly different weights. About three quarters of 1 percent of the whole—that is to say of this 140-pound example—consists of the atoms that have an atomic weight of 235. A little more than 99 percent of the whole consists of the uranium atoms that have an atomic weight of 238. These two sister uranium atoms have different characteristics and capacities. They can be separated from each other to perform their different functions. When all the uranium atoms in the 140-pound cube you saw are so separated, the 235 atoms will be about one cubic inch in size and will weigh about one pound. They are represented by the little cube I now hold before you. The 238 atoms represented by the cube now in my hand will be almost the size of the original cube—because only one cubic inch of mass, represented by the little cube, has been taken out of the original quantity.

The atoms used to be considered the smallest things possible. In fact, however, they consist of a grouping together of a number of subatomic particles, most of which have positive or negative electrical charges and are bound together as a unit. The uranium atom is not only the heaviest of all atoms but it is also the most complex. Uranium metal seems mighty firm and hard. So does the rock in which the ore is found. Nevertheless, the uranium atom is in reality mostly fluff or space. In the center of the atom is a core or nucleus which can be compared to the sun in our solar system. Around this nucleus, many subatomic particles—for the most part electrons—swing in a regular pattern, just as the planets swing about our sun. Comparatively, there is more space, many, many times over, between the nucleus of the atom and its satellite particles than there is space in the heavens between our sun and the various planets.

Practically all the weight or mass of the atom is in its core or nucleus. If you could shuck away and throw into space all parts of the atoms that make up the earth except their nuclei, the earth would lose very little in weight, but it would shrink in size from about 8,000 miles in diameter to about 1,000 feet. The fluff has disappeared but the weight remains. If nuclei could be gathered together the size of a drop of water, they would weigh about two million tons.

In other words, the weight of the mass is in the nucleus of the uranium atom, and it is a part, but only a part, of this mass that we are converting into energy by the process of fission.

What is this process? The nucleus of the uranium atom consists mostly of protons and neutrons bound together. When an extra neutron from a source outside the atom enters the atom and in its flight hits the nucleus, that nucleus splits and the atom shatters. There are such outside, sort of free-wheeling neutrons and the way has been found whereby enough of them can be made to penetrate the 235 atom and start the trigger mechanism known as fissioning. Nearly all the fragments of this shattered 235 uranium atom regroup themselves into new lighter weight atoms, but some part of the mass of the nucleus is released as radiations and energy. Another strange thing happens. In this process of splitting and regrouping of the pieces of one shattered uranium atom, a couple of extra neutrons that were embedded in and a part of the nucleus that was split are released to fly off on their own as sort of orphans or spare parts. If in their flight away from the shattered parts, just one of such released neutrons hits the nucleus of another 235 uranium atom, such atom in turn splits or fissions. This repetition of fissioning is called chain reaction, because starting with the splitting of one atom by one neutron, other atoms are split. If more than one of these released free-wheeling neutrons that are freed by the splitting of the first atom hit and split other 235 nuclei, and each one so split releases two or three more neutrons to do the same thing again, and this goes on and on, it is clear that the results build up very quickly in a cumulative compound-interest sort of way. If the build-up of this chain reaction in a so-called critical mass of 235 uranium atoms is very fast, we have the explosive bomb. If the build-up is slow, we have heat. The speed can be moderated. In either event, we also have many radioactive emanations, some of which are short-lived and some long-lived. They can be destructive to life but some of them, properly controlled, can also be very beneficial.

That, in a nutshell, is the ABC of creation of nuclear energy. It is too simplified to be technically precise or complete, but it is accurate enough to understand generally what is happening in this atomic age and why uranium is a new treasure of the West. In effect, the single neutron from an outside source, when added to the center of the fissionable uranium atom, acts like a trigger or match. Perhaps one more fact should be added. It has to do with the 238 uranium atoms—the 139 pounds of the 140-pound cube.

These 238 atoms won't fission when struck by a neutron. Instead, the neutrons will be absorbed. The absorption causes a metamorphosis. A part of the absorbing mass is changed into plutonium. Plutonium in turn is fissionable, just like the uranium 235 atoms. When one pound of 235 atoms is used to bombard 238 atoms and more than one pound of plutonium results, we end up with more fissionable material than we started with.

This is now being done. It sounds almost like perpetual motion. It is called "breeding." Already in this way—by breeding—the scientists have multiplied by more than twice the effective recoverable energy from the little one-pound, one-inch cube of 235. How far this breeding can go, no one yet knows; certainly considerably farther than it has to date, but probably far short of making fissionable the whole of the 139-pound cube of 238 uranium atoms.

The products of fissioning of the uranium atom have numerous peacetime uses which are growing constantly. The radiation products are today used in medicine by thousands of institutions for diagnostic and clinical work. They may in fact be the great white hope with respect to early detection and most effective treatment of cancer. An entirely new food processing industry may and probably will be built up around radioactive treatment of meat, fruit and other foods. In industry, new plastics and new metal alloys are being developed, and more than a thousand industrial firms are using in various ways the short- or long-lived rays or isotopes that are created when the uranium 235 atom (or its counterpart, plutonium) bursts into fragments. Thus what were originally considered the poisonous wastes or ashes of fission are becoming valuable by-products. Perhaps in time these manifold particular uses, standing alone, will make uranium short in quantity without any military needs.

But the big mass use for uranium that I foresee in the near future is in the production of heat for creation of electricity in our public utility central power plants.

As I have said, the fissioning of uranium produces heat. Fuel for the production of heat is used in this country in vast and increasing amounts, mostly in the form of coal, oil and gas. Uranium will compete with these conventional fuels when it will give the customer more applied heat per dollar of cost than such customer can get in other ways.

This cubic inch of uranium 235 converts itself through fissioning into 37 billion British Thermal Units. Such a large figure, standing by itself, means little. But it is as much heat as one can get through the burning of about 1,500 tons of coal or about 7,000 barrels of oil. That's a great punch for a cubic inch to pack. With the progress to date in "breeding," the 140-pound cube of natural uranium can give us usable heat equal to more than 3,000 tons of coal or about 15,000 barrels of oil. For that much coal or oil available for use under the boilers, the utility company would have to pay in the neighborhood of $30,000. The mine owner gets for the ore that produces this 140-pound cube of natural uranium something on the order of $1,000. It is apparent, therefore, that if there were no intervening costs between the ore as it reaches the mill for concentration and the fissionable atoms at consumers' point of use for heat, uranium would right now competitively undercut the coal and oil several times over. But there are many such intervening costs—for refining, for separation, for construction and operation of nuclear reactors, and for the chemical processing of the uranium from time to time while the original inventory or charge is being fissioned and used.

The average operating cost only of generating electricity in central station steam plants in the United States is on the order of three mills a kilowatt hour. When other than operating costs are taken into account, such as interest and depreciation on and investment in generating equipment, and taxes, such average generating cost for the United States is about seven and one half mills per kilowatt hour.

Even now, at present costs of the usable uranium, the operating costs of generating electricity with nuclear energy are substantially below the operating costs of generation with conventional fuels. Such operating costs with nuclear fuel are as low as one or two mills per kilowatt hour. But the investment costs for nuclear reactors, for the original stock of nuclear fuel (which is almost like buying an inventory of coal or oil to last the life of the plant), and similar items are substantially more than in the case of the conventional present-day modern coal, oil or gas plant. With all items of operating and investment cost included and lumped together, and when large-sized electric generating plants are being considered, we are on the verge of a break-even point competitively between generation with nuclear energy and generation with conventional fuels. But the development of atomic fuel for power plants is only in the expensive horse-and-buggy stage. Costs of nuclear fuel are coming down. Costs of conventional fuels will go up with passage of time. Already in this country a half dozen power plants which will use nuclear fuel are in the course of construction or are projected. In England, where generating costs are a trifle higher than in this country, numerous nuclear power plants are in the initial stage of development.

Now, what can all this mean to our infant uranium industry? Plenty. Let's consider a few statistics.

The population of the United States is growing at a rate of about 1.8 percent per year, and this growth is cumulative. Even though the rate slows down a bit, a population approaching 230,000,000 can be expected by the year 1975. Modern civilization is based on the use of energy, and the use of energy is increasing at a far greater rate than population. We today have about 100 million kilowatts of central station electric power capacity in the United States. It is forecast by the experts in this field that we will have 300 million kilowatts by 1975. This is a three-fold growth in electric output while the population is increasing by less than 100 percent. I have studied the statistics carefully relating to this growth of electric energy and the use in this connection of nuclear fuel. It is my opinion that by 1960 we will have at least four million kilowatts of electrical capacity constructed or in course of building that will be fueled with uranium, and that this figure will grow cumulatively until it will reach not less than forty million kilowatts by 1975. After that time, practically all new plants will be nuclear fueled. That is because presently available water power sites will have been developed and conventional fuels will have risen in cost, while the costs of refining and packaging uranium for heat use will have decreased. Therefore, nuclear fuel will be the most economical in nearly all cases after 1975.

So far as I can ascertain, we don't yet have nearly enough uranium in reserve in the ground in this country to meet such a growing and very imposing demand.

We will need to mine millions of tons of ore per year for this one purpose alone, and we will need reserves of uranium ore for years ahead, because nuclear-fueled power plants which, when built, will be in operation for a decade or more cannot be based on hopes concerning a continuing fuel supply. Cheap power—and nuclear fuel is the way we will keep power cheap—is most important to our economy. A saving of one mill per kilowatt hour in costs of generation will mean a billion dollars a year or more in our over-all economy.

We hear that conventional fuels like coal and oil, while growing more expensive as time passes, will also grow more efficient and will not be eliminated by nuclear fuel. We also hear that fusion—which is represented by creation of heat through the building up of lighter atoms like hydrogen and lithium rather than the breaking down of the heavy uranium atom—will come into a leading role in the nuclear era. We also hear that the sun's heat will be directly harnessed. We hear that thorium can be made fissionable and may take the place of uranium. Finally, we hear that uranium will be found almost everywhere and that there can be an oversupply.

As I have stated, I hope and expect that much more uranium will be found. It is needed. How could we ever have built the mechanized age with its automobiles, tractors and the like if we had not discovered vast supplies of oil to last for years in the future? To build a power industry around nuclear reactors we must have reserves of nuclear fuel for cumulative needs over many future years. Thorium can be used and in time will be used to supplement uranium. But our national research and national investment are in uranium. It does not seem to me that we will shift in the middle of the stream to start over again with a new element which, in its most workable form and greater quantities, lies beyond our national borders. The hydrogen bomb can well displace the uranium bomb for purposes of national defense where cost is of secondary consideration. But my information is that fusion for purposes of controlled energy in industry is many years away at best. As to conventional fuels, they will not be displaced. Electric plants built to use coal or oil will work out their useful lives. New plants, however, will more and more use nuclear fuel. It is good that we have this new fuel coming along. Otherwise, with three times as much electricity to generate twenty years from now as we have today, our costs of generation would be high. And it is cheap energy that has made America move forward to its present high standard of living.

We should not be dependent for our nuclear fuel on the import of uranium from abroad. Bear in mind in this connection that with uranium, the cost of generation of electricity will be about the same all over the world because the cost of transporting a few of these little cubes of treasure is negligible. That means that the rest of the world will have increasing electrical growth probably paralleling our own, and an increasing standard of living to match such power growth. These countries will have use for their own uranium at home or will have other competing markets. England, for example, must import uranium for all the power plants she is projecting.

Let's think for a moment in terms of Salt Lake City. This beautiful and well laid-out city has grown from about 100,000 population to about 200,000 since I started to work here. But the population of the West will grow from here on faster than the population of the country as a whole, and Utah, with her uranium treasure, should grow faster than the West as a whole. I expect that Salt Lake City will have a population in excess of one million by 1975. The city fathers in charge of planning and their sons had better prepare for this.

Let's look at it from another standpoint. When Salt Lake City has a million population, Utah Power and Light will need substantially more than five times its present power capacity to serve its then customers in its present operating territory. But even so, a dozen cubes, more or less, of uranium 235 the size of this little one-inch cube would fuel such plants for the greater part of a full day.

Utah, I believe, has today about forty million barrels of oil in reserve in the ground. Such oil in reserve is worth roughly $1.00 a barrel in place, or $40,000,000. A million tons of fairly good commercial grade of uranium ore in place in the ground has a value equal to all this oil reserve. And I know of uranium ore bodies in Utah of mining grade that aggregate several million tons of ore. In other words, uranium far outweighs oil as Utah's natural resource even now. And each day the value of this natural treasure is increasing through new discoveries and new processes of concentration and refinement that reduce the cost to the customer of the final usable product.

In my study of the commercial future of uranium, I concluded that if the military uses for atomic power should cease entirely and if there were no uses for uranium except as fuel in public utility power plants, we would need, starting tomorrow morning and running to capacity, more milling capacity than we now have in order to meet this single requirement. I can only conclude

147

that the future is a bright one. The horizons seem unlimited.

I am glad when each new uranium discovery is reported. We need the reserves on which soundly to build the future. So long as such a small portion of the cost of the nuclear heat that uranium will release goes to the mine owner, with such a substantial part of that small portion being absorbed by mining costs and depletion, I have no fear of any harmful reduction in price for ore.

I am pleased when a Charlie Steen or a Joe Cooper or a Vernon Pick strikes it rich. That means that many others will try and follow in their paths, which in turn means development and growth of the uranium industry and our entire national economy. Of course, many who try will lose. How much value will come out of the ground in relation to what is put into the ground in time and money, I do not know. That is the gamble in all new enterprises. I hope the return will be great. It should be. Profits come from taking risks. And the men or group of speculators who, with wide-open eyes, risk the loss of their stake are entitled to extremely good rewards when they hit pay dirt.

Salt Lake City has the lead in the uranium field today in many ways. It could be the uranium capital of tomorrow, and it is a very bright tomorrow that I visualize.

So I now salute you in your onward march, and thank you for listening to me.

INTRODUCTION

TO XVII

In August 1956 in New Orleans I addressed the members of the Air Force Association at their symposium with respect to industry's role relating to scientific and engineering manpower.

The surge of technical and scientific training in Russia had been giving me concern. I was urged to make this particular presentation by a few of our leading scientists who were also concerned about our own lag in these fields.

XVII

~~~~~~~~~~~~~~~~

The general subject for discussion today is "Manpower in the Jet-Atomic Age." I have been asked to speak on "Industry's Role Relative to Scientific and Technical Manpower."

Whatever reason the officers of the Air Force Association had in selecting me for this particular talk, I am honored and pleased. The reason was not because of any direct connection of mine with the defense industry. I have had no such connection since my Convair days. Since the early days of the Air Force Association, I have believed in its objectives and have had satisfaction in some association with its activities, its officers, and its friends.

It has been my unusual lot over the last forty years to go into and out of many different businesses in a number of different industries both here and abroad. I have been at various times deep in the electric industry, the aircraft industry, air transport, motion pictures, banks, stores, oil and uranium. The differences between these various industries and subdivisions are glaringly apparent. But there are inward similarities. The X factor common to all is important as bearing on American progress and prosperity as a whole. With my background as stated, perhaps I can see the forest better than the individual trees. It is from this position that I will add my brief remarks to the general discussion.

Man has made fairly continuous progress for himself ever

since discovery and applied use of fire and the wheel. But there have been long lulls and fast jumps. The industrial revolution started one of those fast jumps forward. The industrial revolution started in England, not too long before the Wright brothers made the first powered airplane flight. It spread to Europe and to America. It then caught on to a lesser degree in India and some other Eastern countries, including particularly Japan where it flourished until Japan felt strong enough to challenge our supremacy. The German leaders acknowledged after both world wars that they were defeated by our American industrial capacity.

And now the industrial revolution has taken hold in Russia. It had its beginnings there during or shortly after World War I. The industrial growth in Russia has been rapid in recent years. Russia started in this respect, let it be remembered, with the aid of our own machines, equipment and know-how. Let it also be remembered that we have a national policy of aiding through our Point IV program and otherwise the so-called backward nations on their way to industrial self-sufficiency.

Man's desires for more things—for a higher standard of living—seem insatiable. The raw materials for these more and better things are dug up mostly from the earth's crust which our progenitors trod naked in search for daily meat. First, we had to dig only lightly to get rich grades of ores and then oil and coal for heat. These things were fabricated and refined. But now we have to mine deeper and be satisfied with lower-grade ores. That additional effort and cost must be offset by improved technology. In this process brawn has given way to brainpower. Footpower has given way to horsepower and horsepower has given way to megawatts.

Study all the nations today and you will find that their industrial progress and standard of living tie directly into the amount of mechanical energy used per capita. The abundance and cheapness of electrical and other forms of mechanical energy are what count. High wages do not hold us back if backed up by cheaply operated machines in mass production. For that reason I do not go along with the fears of some that Russia will take our world trade away from us—that she will do so because her laborer gets only about one sixth the wage we pay in the United States. We use more than six times the energy per capita that is used per capita in Russia.

If cheap and abundant mechanical energy is the thing—and it is—then we are entering a new era which is being superimposed on the industrial age. It is the atomic era. The fissioning of the uranium atom has brought us an abundant source of heat that will keep our presently cheap energy cost from rising in future years. It is a scientific, a technological advance with outstanding impact. But there is a reverse side of the coin. Atomic energy will also be abundant and cheap all around the world in places where coal and oil are now too expensive in energy value to transport and use. The handmaidens of atomic energy—jet propulsion, electronics and automatic controls—are also in the cast of principals in this show of tomorrow's life. Yes, and weather modification also. I forecast that as a result of these brain children the present centers of industrial power and leadership, the present places of high standards of living have no monopoly. We will lose our place of pre-eminence unless we take heed and do the necessary things.

The threat to our leadership is great. There is no point in expecting Russia to slow up her industrialization or, for that matter, any other country. Our job is to keep ahead of the others. What I have to say on this point adds up to more and better use of scientists and engineers. The free world is in contest with communism on the economic front even as it is on the military front. The contest is breaking out openly right now. The size and quality of the technical and scientific elements on either side will form a very real and major element in any final decision in the struggle between communism and our own way of life.

We are moving into the age of automatic controls—more output with fewer man hours. Intelligent direction of the controls therefore becomes all-important. Pure basic science must be the fountainhead for all this. Applied science and technology must follow through in top, all-important spots. The countries that develop during the next few years the greatest scientists and engineers—the most and the best—are the countries that will be the foremost, the most powerful and the most prosperous in this new jet-atomic age.

In this regard it is now generally recognized, as this very symposium implies, that the United States is in real danger of falling behind the Soviet Union in the critical fields of educating, training and the use of adequate numbers of scientists, engineers and technicians.

The Russians noticed some years back where we were strong and they were weak. They started to copy our elements of strength, and with a vengeance. You have heard the statistics today from other qualified speakers. I will not repeat them. They show clearly a critical situation. I will only say that they show that in four decades our Russian competitors have almost overtaken us quantitatively in the scientific and technical fields, and will pass us within the next five years if we don't get very busy. They show that we are graduating fewer engineers and scientists than five years ago, while the Russians are graduating many more. They show that only one out of five high school pupils with capacities for careers in engineering and science graduate from college; that only about 18 percent of these graduates receive degrees in engineering and science, with the percentage steadily dropping. They also show that of all college graduates fewer than 3 percent carry on to a Doctor's degree.

And let's not engage in the wishful thinking that the quality of the Russian scientists and engineers is inferior to our own. We have been doing great technological things, it is true. We were the first to harness the atom, the first to break the sound barrier. We have unequaled television and fine coast-to-coast dial telephones. We have more power steering and drive than most other nations combined. But the Russians have also harnessed the atom and are familiar with the thermonuclear process. Their radar systems in many respects match ours and they also have designed and operated supersonic aircraft. Don't be deluded by the fact that they have not bothered to improve their plumbing or to pave their streets. Realize instead that they may be only doing first things first in meeting their long-range objectives, which objectives have been and are dangerous to us.

How did the Russians make this progress without private initiative and enterprise to impel them—that is to say, under dictatorship? From information afforded me by friends in the scientific and military world, I surmise they turned this trick by careful selection of the fields of technical and scientific endeavor they wanted developed for industrial and war plans; by organized and directed assignment to those fields of the very best talent from youth on by maximum utilization of those talents; by unlimited development funds and facilities for programs within the boundaries of the Soviet plan; and finally, but by no means least, by recognition of the engineer and scientist as a superior individual entitled to respect, prestige and emoluments far beyond what we give them comparatively in our country.

Now what can we do—particularly from industry's point of view—to improve our own situation? Long-range solutions would involve the following: First—better, more intensive teaching of the sciences in our colleges and universities to more students. This involves getting more freshmen into our advanced schools of learning with the preliminary training to qualify them to major in the sciences.

This in turn involves teachers in our primary and secondary schools better qualified to train the youngsters in mathematics, physics, chemistry and the like. Many of the high school teachers are now just a jump ahead of their pupils in these science subjects.

Finally, and most important of all, the children must be intrigued into studying these subjects. Industry can do its share here by supporting the education of teachers through scholarships and grants. Also through the loans of its own personnel as teachers. Also, by minimizing the plundering of colleges and universities of their teaching talent in these critical fields. Instead of hiring top scientists away from their teaching of others, industry might better leave them where they are and hire them as part-time consultants.

When one industrial unit hires scientists away from another industrial unit our over-all national problem is not helped. I have seen a lot of this go on. I saw one electronics company grow to outstanding proportions by this process. Then I saw the process repeated. These activities were disruptive. It is to be hoped they may also have been constructive.

Individuals in industry can also well afford to devote their personal attention to the fiscal and management problems of the secondary schools in the communities in which they live. For us who believe in states' rights (including the field of education), let's not let neglect of teaching become a serious matter of national defense.

Industry might use its renowned imagination in sales technique through advertising and otherwise to impress young Americans —boys and girls—that science when properly taught and understood is interesting and exciting. Here I also believe our scientific friends could help by bringing their imaginations to bear on how we can make algebra and geometry fun for our youngsters. I recently saw a television lecture by Dr. Edward Teller on nuclear energy. It was entertainment of the highest order and instructive. We need more things like this presented to our youth during their impressionable, formative years.

I see plenty of juvenile cowboys and Davey Crocketts running around. There is no future connected with the long rifle or the branding iron. There is an atomic establishment down in the area where Davey Crockett roamed and the cowboy ranges of the West are providing us with uranium. The future fun for these boys and girls will be in converting these parts of the earth's surface into heat and light and medicine and better goods as well as into new flying machines guided by remote control. They should be made to realize it.

And I must not neglect to state that there should be scholarships in abundance for well-qualified students in science, as well as teaching grants. Industry and foundations should, directly with worthy students or through the schools, see that this comes about.

Then I would suggest various means of getting more mileage from the scientific and engineering talent we already have with us in industry. This means better management. At this point I wish to remark that about a third of the scientists and engineers in private industry are on work for the Federal Government, mostly for the Defense Department. Our senior partners, the Armed Services, therefore share the responsibility of better management of the engineers and scientists.

To the lay observer there could at times be a better integrated statement of the development requirements of the Services. There might be less duplications of demand upon scarce talents to invent the same kind of machines to do the same job in the same period of time. As an example, I believe in the ballistic missile field there are multiple efforts. Since these multiple programs must in effect compete with each other for engineering and scientific skills as well as for money facilities and management, one can wonder if all stem from an integrated plan. This particular weapons program is urgent. Might we not have a better chance of acquiring some of these extremely difficult and important weapons *sooner* if we had fewer projects to deal with?

Industry might, with better management, do current tasks with fewer people. When I hear about two thousand or more engineers on an airframe task it impresses me as wastage. Increasingly complex tasks can't be solved by merely increasing numbers of people at work. With 2,000 engineers on a single project, a disturbing number of them must be wasting their technical skills in administrative and other nonengineering tasks.

Scientists should be playing a more active role within the halls of industry. Scientists can render major contributions to quicker and more efficient engineering of a development when appropriately placed in the organization. This way we can get more inventions out of fewer people. I am not speaking now of the role of scientists in laboratories of broad research. I am bringing them out onto the firing line of management.

Engineers and scientists in the organization should be given time to help in the local school educational efforts. They should be given time to do some broad basic thinking—to draw upon areas of physical theory that have been little used until now. For an airplane to travel faster than a rifle bullet for hours on end takes this kind of free-wheeling thinking. Defense against a ballistic missile, which means the invention of a bullet to hit a bullet, requires venturing into unfamiliar realms of science involving collaboration of engineers and scientists.

We called on the scientist heavily during the last war. Many of industry's tasks today are similar in complexity or even greater than those pursued during the war. A scientist in the top echelon of company management, in communication with the company engineers, provides authoritative consultation in his field and a fresh viewpoint from which to evaluate problems. He also can act as professional contact and interpreter with consultants in related fields. He may well interpret technical problems presented by a new product quite differently than an engineer. He may see how technique used in research laboratories elsewhere may be applied to the business in hand, thus avoiding a much broader company research program that would require large numbers of engineers.

There are a number of different ways of integrating within a single organization the scientific and engineering skills and management efforts. None of them may be perfect. All have the objective of tapping all available resources of knowledge inside and outside the organization applicable to the company's problems.

We must, as does our Soviet competition, *utilize* our talents more efficiently. We must also, as does our Soviet competition, *recognize* our talented people more.

Our system at the moment is such that the only chance an engineer or a scientist has for maximum advancement is to get into administration. This may always be partly true, since there will be an increasing requirement for efficient administration in scientific and technical fields. But there should also be opportunity for recognition of superior technical men who are either not qualified for or who are not used in administration. And this recognition should come not only in the form of remuneration and recognition from his chief executive, but from others in his field as well.

Publication in professional journals, presentation of papers, preparation of monographs should be encouraged and supported. This should be so despite the fact that in industry and in particular in a defense industry there are limitations connected with security classification.

We cannot, as the Soviets do, force our bright young people into science. We must attract them into the field. Somehow or other we must establish national and social eminence to a greater degree than we have for our technical and scientific people, if we are to make these areas of enterprise interesting enough to draw and hold a growing number of talented youngsters. Thus, in closing, I come back to our youth again.

In this regard I am mindful of a current experience of a friend of mine, a scientist of international stature. He is bemused by the venture of his thirteen-year-old son, whose IQ is of a high order, and who is naturally enough partial toward mathematical and scientific subjects. The boy's principal interest these days, however, lies in winning a berth on his junior high school football team. Despite the fact the youngster doesn't particularly care for the game of football and, according to his father, has in the last twelve months broken four pairs of thick-lensed spectacles he has to wear, both father and son are agreed the boy will continue his attempt to make the team. This because the boy has already deduced that his life in school will be happier and his acceptance with his fellow students more general if he makes the football team and lives down the suspicion his fellows have of him that he is a highbrow.

That is not an unusual situation, and each of us in his way contributes daily to its continuation. But somehow each of us must bring himself to work toward the day when out of every hundred young Americans who know who Ted Williams and Mickey Mantle are, at least one of them will at the same time know who Edward Teller and Theodore von Karman are.

Point the way how to get more and better mathematics, physics and chemistry taught in our primary and secondary schools—taught to youth keenly interested in these subjects, and you will be showing the way to an America that will *continue* to be pre-eminent and prosperous.

INTRODUCTION

TO XVIII

The Lotos Club of New York honored Mr. Henry Luce and his wife, Clare Boothe Luce, with a state dinner on December 11, 1958, and I was honored by being requested to make one of the three speeches. Mine was to bring out the financial aspects of Mr. Luce's career with the family of magazines made up principally of *Life, Time* and *Fortune.* It is a financial story few people know about, and for that reason, among others, I choose to include my remarks in this collection.

XVIII

~~~~~~~~~~~~~~~~~~~~~

Time, if fruitfully employed, leads to Fortune, and with both Time and Fortune one becomes almost assured of an interesting Life. Mr. Henry Luce neatly tied these three ingredients of success together, and in the order named.

I was around with watchful eyes while this process was unfolding—one of the business wonders of our century.

Although birth occurred for Mr. Luce out in China some years earlier, *Time* really started to run for him in 1923. How well I remember this date because it was when I started Atlas Corporation.

Fortune was spawned by *Time* in 1930 and I was practically in on the "borning." On Sunday evenings in those days Mr. Luce had groups in for supper and discussions at his club, and I was privileged to be among his guests on some of these occasions. Discussions covered the widest range, yet they always seemed to have a common denominator. All had a bearing in some way on the way Mr. Luce would shape himself to shape the future of his publications.

What a future was before Mr. Luce and these publications at that time! A future, up to now, to be equaled only by what is still ahead.

Magazines are by no means merely paper and print. At least some aren't.

Behind the researchers and the writers, behind the photographers and the art directors is the magazine's creator who by his intellect, desires, vigor, fortitude and ambitions gives the magazine its quality of lifeblood, its artistic and intellectual hormones, its personality.

You see the creator in Mr. Luce. I have seen this too. But as a financial man I have seen more.

Picture Henry Luce and his co-founder, Britton Hadden, back in 1922 relying largely on their better-heeled Yale classmates to raise through stock the $100,000 needed to start the publication of *Time.* They only raised $36,000 at the time, but started publication anyway.

I won't take you down all the by-paths of stock bonuses and redemptions, stock splits and dividends since that time. I'll just say this much which should be plenty. The individual who invested one hundred dollars in Time, Inc. at the start and never disturbed his holding has today, in dividends received and market value of stock, more than forty-two thousand dollars.

A hundred-dollar investment like this is a good way to keep on the high road leading directly away from the poorhouse and to the gates of the Palace of Croesus.

Time from that small beginning is now really an enormous investment trust which has, besides *Fortune* and *Life,* several other robust picture and print children. For the steady diet of these children, *Time* has large pulp and paper companies as well as research laboratories for graphic arts and vast presses and printing plants. For their housing *Time,* as a partner with Rockefeller Center, has the 48-story building in New York besides a big office building in Chicago. Almost as frosting on the cake, *Time* has broadcasting stations in a half-dozen cities.

The financial community knows well the impact of Mr. Luce. *Time* gives a report quick and current. For a full analysis of business and industry we turn to *Fortune.* And we can only be astounded at the phenomenon of a magazine like *Life* whose single issue (according to last week's press) can, through the inadvertent inclusion of a loose card, bring down from the Government an additional postage charge of a million dollars.

It was not all a one-way street. Remember that *Fortune,* a kind of luxury product at a dollar a copy, was started in 1930, when the depression was just digging in. *Life,* when it was started, nearly died of too much success. It had geared its advertising rate for the first year to a circulation of 250,000 and the circulation climbed to more than a million. The advertisers got that additional coverage free. It was a growing pain of proportion for *Time* but the child *Life* went on to become a giant.

But it is not of dollars I mean principally to speak tonight. My emphasis is on the man. And what a man is Henry Luce.

But also on the top of the pinnacle is his distinguished wife, Clare Boothe Luce. The first time I felt the force of her intellect was back in the thirties at the home of the late Condé Nast. I heard her give a penetrating analysis of communism that I have never heard bettered since. Whether in the drawing room or in the writing studio, in the halls of Congress or in the corridors of diplomacy, she is always at her brilliant and beautiful best. Unlike a flaming meteor she does not get burned up by entry into the "down to earth" atmosphere. She is constantly in orbit.

America can be proud of this couple. They have left an imperishable mark on a generation and more. The Lotos Club does well to place them on its scroll of immortals. I feel privileged to join in honoring them.

INTRODUCTION

TO XIX

Eleven years ago I helped organize the Arthritis and Rheumatism Foundation and I have been its chairman ever since. Many speeches have I made on its behalf.

I think one of them should be in this collection and I have selected for the purpose my talk in June 1959 at Washington, D. C., before the Pan-American Congress on Rheumatic Diseases. At that meeting, acting on behalf of the American Rheumatism Association and the Arthritis and Rheumatism Foundation, I presented plaques to Senator Lister Hill and Representative John E. Fogarty for their leadership in Congress on behalf of medical research and education.

XIX

A few years ago at Atlantic City, the American Rheumatism Association was gracious enough to confer on me an honorary membership. Otherwise I would feel lonelier than I do up here surrounded as I am by doctors and scientists. Among so many distinguished M.D.'s and Ph.D.'s, I am distinctly a lay member of the flock, but as such I share with you your deep concern about the mystery and challenge of arthritis and rheumatism. My interest in these diseases is not entirely theoretical. It developed the hard way as a painfully personal experience.

When I was stricken years ago and traveled from medical center to medical center in search of health, I learned that little was known about the cause or cure of arthritis, and that treatment was almost as varied as the doctors involved.

All this was most frustrating. But progress has been made since then. Such progress is great related to the starting point. But it is only a start along the hard road to success in eliminating the disease or group of diseases or conditions known as arthritis and rheumatism. As you have passed milepost after milepost with greater speed, the end of the road is nearer and surer. And by the end of the road I mean the accomplishment of the mission. The vast amount of new material presented at this Congress is most heartening. The number of skilled doctors and scientists who are working in this field is impressive, and I clearly sense the stimulation you have derived from these presentations.

Research seemed to me ten years ago to be essential if the cause of arthritis and rheumatism were to be discovered and the more effective treatment and cure of sufferers brought about. It was a problem the solution of which seemed worthy of a "crash program," considering the scores of millions of people afflicted, and the suffering and economic waste involved. I discovered at the time that only about forty thousand dollars was being spent a year on research in the entire United States. The arthritic was the forgotten man.

Tonight I am here representing the Arthritis and Rheumatism Foundation, a national voluntary health agency with a network of about sixty chapters throughout the United States. This Foundation, which combines as partners laymen like myself with physicians and scientists like you, was created ten years ago to serve the purposes of research, patient care and professional education. A group of leaders in the American Rheumatism Association asked me to help in the formation of this Foundation. I became its chairman at the start, a position which I have proudly held down to date. The purpose of the Arthritis and Rheumatism Foundation is to raise funds from the general public and to expend them wisely, according to the best medical and scientific advice available. Ever since its creation, the Arthritis and Rheumatism Foundation has enjoyed the valuable counsel of the American Rheumatism Association. In turn, the Association has received Foundation grants for the conduct of its administrative and scientific affairs.

It has been a decade of great growth for both organizations. The growth, as Dr. Bunim stated earlier in the week, has been "in number and in maturity." In that first year our Foundation raised a few thousand dollars from a few people. This year we have raised a few million dollars from several hundred thousand people. But what we are raising is far too small considering the stupendously important job to be done. These funds, along with the help from the Government that I will refer to in a moment, have provided immeasurably more clinics in the country. Rheumatology is being taught today in our medical schools to a higher degree than in the past; a flood of scientific publications and lay literature is reaching the patients and clinics; fellows are being supported while training for research and thereafter in research; and ever more physicians in general practice are becoming skilled in diagnosing and treating arthritis and the other rheumatic diseases.

While there is occasionally a great and far-reaching medical discovery, almost by accident, most of the progress comes from close, hard and well-coordinated research by trained experts. I have in mind in this connection, among others, the antibiotics, cortisone, the polio vaccine, hypertension drugs, anticoagulants, as well as the pain-killers. Research pays big dividends. It has in recent years made the trip through life of longer duration and more pleasant. In the last fifteen years, since medical research has received such growing support, the results of research have saved about two million lives of people who would otherwise have died. Research has entirely eradicated some diseases that had high mortality rates. Research will also put arthritis and the rheumatic diseases into this gone-but-not-forgotten class where they belong. I believe this will come about. I believe you people are well on your way toward such result.

For these encouraging developments, the Foundation and the Association cannot claim sole credit. The expanding efforts of both organizations have been greatly reinforced by the creation and activities of the National Institute of Arthritis and Metabolic Diseases. That is one of the several institutions of health within the framework of the United States Department of Health supported by Congressional appropriation. This is both right and good. The preamble to the Constitution of our Republic stated that the common welfare of our people is one of the prime purposes of government. And health is the essence of common welfare.

As a member of the National Advisory Council of the Institute for Arthritis and Metabolic Diseases I have been privileged to witness the rapidly increasing development of the Institute's program in the field of research and training, both at Bethesda, here in the Washington area and in our medical schools.

Let me illustrate my point with just a figure or two. I mentioned earlier that just before our Arthritis and Rheumatism Foundation was formed only about $40,000 was being spent for research on arthritis in the entire country. The Institute was formed a little after our Foundation, but in its first years of operations it granted $131,000 for research in arthritis alone. During the present fiscal year the amount spent on research in arthritis alone has grown to $4,000,000.

Money for these various health institutes for research in the various health fields comes from Congress by appropriation. Congress is recognizing the need for research in the interest of the welfare of our people. Congress is realizing that research pays off in a big way in terms of health and general economy. In 1946 the appropriation for all the institutes of health aggregated only $3,500,000. In this current session of Congress the appropriation bill for the national institutes as passed by the House of Representatives exceeds $344,000,000. This is a hundredfold increase in little over a decade. It is still too little, but more will come, I am sure, with the passage of time. Three hundred and forty-four million dollars is a lot of money, but it is still small compared with research within the Armed Services. And it is no more than what we the people pay out annually for chewing gum, lipstick, face powder and make-up, and only a fraction of our expenditure for alcohol or tobacco. The annual research cost in the field of arthritis is still small compared with the cost of developing a single new type of airplane or engine or of giving two monkeys a ride in the nose cone of a missile. In fact it is less than we spend on sending get-well cards to the sick.

But the sums of money spent through these institutes have saved many lives and have lengthened the life span of all of us. The efforts made possible by this money have helped to mend bodies and souls. The expenditures to date have formed a splendid scientific reservoir of skilled manpower and tools on which we and our children can draw for better health and happiness.

Our representatives in Congress acting on behalf of all of us have made the program possible. But our senators and representatives do not act in these matters by common impulse. It takes leadership. A program of such vast significance needs men who not only understand the need, but who can forcibly present such need and interpret it in terms understandable to all of us.

We are most fortunate to have two such men with us here tonight, Senator Lister Hill of Alabama and Representative John E. Fogarty of Rhode Island. I value the opportunity to honor them here and now with joint awards of the American Rheumatism Association and the Arthritis and Rheumatism Foundation—the first of this kind ever given.

INTRODUCTION

TO XX

My preacher father had a rule that each son, prior to graduation from college, would address my father's parishioners from the pulpit. My three older brothers did so, but I escaped this experience because at the time of my graduation my father was a thousand miles away and no longer preaching.

Forty-six years later I was invited to deliver the Baccalaureate Sermon at Northland College, Ashland, Wisconsin. In accepting I believed I was fulfilling that long-neglected duty to my father.

During the intervening years I had thought a great deal about religion and immortality, but not to the point of having conclusions I was willing to express. Such as these conclusions finally are as of now, they are set forth in the accompanying sermon, delivered June 5, 1960.

Freedom of expression was granted me at time of invitation but I was fearful that what I had to say might not go well with the trustees and faculty of a college affiliated with the Congregational Church. But my thoughts were well received. I was surprised by the great number of people who shared my views.

My wife did not know my religious views. She did not know what I was going to say. She listened while seated near me on the rostrum, where later she was to deliver the Commencement Address. Afterward she said that, during the first part of my talk, she thought I was headed for Hell, but that I managed before the end to pull myself back from the brink and re-establish myself as a man with a soul.

XX

A few years back I accepted an invitation to address our Western Mining Congress on the subject of nuclear energy. I
was engaged at the time in mining uranium ore but I knew very
little about how that rock became converted into energy either
for atomic bombs or for peaceful applications. I agreed to make
that speech in order to force myself to learn something about the
uranium atom, nuclear fission, chain reaction and other related
things.

It was much the same with me when I, a layman steeped in
business, was audacious enough a year ago to agree to deliver
today's Baccalaureate Sermon and therefore to speak concerning
religion and spiritual concepts. Since my youth, I have engaged
in an inner conflict concerning my attitudes and beliefs, and I
wished by self-analysis, contemplation and coordination of
thoughts to reach conclusions.

Blessed is the person to whom faith cometh early in life. And
such a person is my wife, Jacqueline Cochran, whom you will
hear later. Our roles for today might well have been reversed.
With some confidence I could have given in a commencement
address some of my lifelong experiences dealing with temporal
affairs. She, on the other hand, is a shining living example of pure
unadulterated faith in the divine and in immortality. Thus "sus-
tained and soothed by an unfaltering trust," she has followed the

highways and byways of life without fear and with a sureness of purpose.

It's reasonable to assume—as probably your President Gus Turbeville did—that I, born and raised in the parsonage, the child of a devout mother and a Methodist preacher father, should have been from the start a pillar of faith. But it was not so. It was just the contrary. I was a doubter from the start. I memorized the prayers, the psalms and the hymns. But it was a routine. I was doing what was expected of me. And when I compared the moaning of the faithful in the church with the apparent happiness of the gang down at the drugstore corner, the sinners seemed to me to have the best of it.

My greatest trouble was that I could not believe literally in the words of the Bible, although I kept this disbelief to myself. I could not harmonize the image of a God of goodness with a Jehovah, jealous, revengeful and full of wrath. What I read about the iniquities and harshness of the ancient multitudes caused me to think that the Creator should not have rested on the seventh day, because His task was not completed. He had placed mortals on earth without instilling in them principles of purity and peace. Jonah's sojourn in the belly of a whale was to me just another fish story. As for Adam and Eve, I thought it all wrong that such a wonderful creature as woman should have a rib as ancestor. I resented having to read aloud the long chapters in the Bible dealing with dull genealogy; I resented the monotony of sermons; and I resented the prohibition against whistling or being my happy self on Sundays.

And so, come eighteen, when I left home for school, I also definitely split away from the atmosphere of parsonage and church. I was at least an agnostic and at times I thought I approached the portals of atheism, although I know now this was not so. In any event, for years I never entered a church.

But with age also comes better understanding.

At school I was somewhat surprised to find that most of my classmates, although away from home atmosphere, were nevertheless religious. In classroom I learned, possibly without appreciating its significance, that almost all of mankind is religious and has been in one form or another ever since given the power of contemplation. I learned that the Christian religion alone, which is only one of several living religions with the same basic concept, encompasses about a third of the earth's enormous population; that England's Magna Carta, France's Declaration of the Rights of Man, and America's Declaration of Independence all acknowledge God; that sessions of our Congress are opened with prayer; that our coinage bears the words "In God we trust"; that our cities and villages are studded with steeples and spires denoting places of worship; and that in hundreds of thousands of assemblages of many kinds, millions of people in our land every day give thanks to God and ask for divine guidance.

I asked myself whether so many people could be wrong and only a few like myself could be right. Was it some ego on my part that kept me aloof from the beliefs of the multitude? I don't know. But I still remained an isolationist, wanting proof.

Science, in fact, is almost as young as religion is old. The physical scientist is not a magician or the leader of a cult. He is usually a very studious, hard-working person in a particular field of the physical. His life is centered in the material. No wonder many scientists are materialists.

We are in the full bloom of a scientific era. What the scientists tell us today and that we fully accept would have been considered scientific heresy not much more than a few score of decades ago. Because of this accent on materialism, science and religion are supposed to be in conflict. And yet, with science surging upward, religion has also spread and grown. The conflict may not be as real as many suppose.

I am not even a junior grade scientist of any sort. I have several as close friends and I am occasionally therefore exposed to their views. I also, while traveling the path of life, have browsed occasionally along the edges of certain fields of science. Just a little. But each time my mind has been opened to greater understanding. Each time my course of thinking has been altered or tempered to some degree.

Strangely enough, the findings of science and the views of certain scientists brought me back to the basic beliefs of my parents in the divine order of things and the immortality of the nonphysical inner side of man, represented by spirit, soul or mind, whichever term one chooses to use. I choose to use the term "mind."

If I have anything helpful to offer to any of you today it is because what I say comes from a man driven away from religion in his youth by the Bible and brought back in his maturity by science.

The minutes at my disposal are too few to paint my thoughts except with a very broad brush and also with apologies to all scientists and theologians within earshot.

It is with wonder and awe that I view the inorganic world, whether I look outward to the universe that stretches in every direction without end or inward to the minute atom and its subparts. This inorganic world of which our earth is but a speck had a beginning. The astronomers and physicists by different approaches reach about the same time, several billion years ago, when the universe was born. The countless billions of heavenly bodies that whirl about through space have determinable and predictable courses; and furthermore, the universe is expanding at a regular and progressive rate. Reverse this process of expansion to one of contraction and there comes a time when all parts of the universe were together. That's the astronomer's approach.

The physicists deal with the few basic elements found in varying degrees in all masses of the universe that can come under analysis; and with the ascertainable rates of deterioration or conversion of these elements, a point in time is reached when it appears as conclusive that a central mass or pool of material and energy fractured into its billions of parts which then started their slow process of degradation. Such a time coincides quite closely with the astronomers' time found for nature's birthday.

Ever since that birthday the universe has been slowly wearing out. In time so distant in the future as almost to escape human comprehension, all inorganic mass will have reached the point of inert equilibrium or stabilization, with all energy dissipated, with total obscurity and absolute cold.

But in the meantime the orderliness of the parts of the universe in their long continued turning and coursing is to me full of implications. What a dramatic and creative act it was when this universe was set in motion. And in its regular movements it seems as if a supreme conductor must be directing the harmony of the heavens.

As wonderful as is the universe of stars and planets, it is paralleled in wonder by the atom. For a long time considered the smallest unit in nature, it has been split during recent years and the universe within the single atom was discovered. The subparticles of some atoms are numerous. These subparticles wheel about each other, or, more accurately, around the nucleus of their atom, at terrific speeds and always in obedience to certain physical laws. The atom is mostly space just as the universe is mostly space. A piece of hardest steel or a granite rock is mostly spongy fluff, alive with motion.

The same orderliness goes on within the atom as goes on within the outer universe. The laws of inorganic matter are being obeyed. I sense the same unseen guidance at work.

The atom and the subparts of the atom cannot be seen, but our scientists know the atom exists and know its characteristics and the characteristics of its subparts. Their minds can, with justification, comprehend and appreciate what they cannot see.

The organic world is even more wonderful and awe-inspiring than the inorganic. The biologists, paleontologists and other experts in the fields of living sciences have told us much.

When organic life first started on earth, no one knows. Whether it started with the first living cell, or long before then with an amorphous matter as some scientists believe, or whether the seeds of life were here from the start, it seems certain that evolution started at the same time.

And the interesting feature of organic evolution is that it proceeds with increasing organized complexity and differentiation and with trend upward, whereas the inorganic world seems slowly, regularly devoluting, or moving downward toward equilibrium.

Science has not been able to find any satisfactory bridge between living and nonliving matter. Life cannot be explained by chance, according to scientists who have considered the subject carefully, and I believe them. Life had a start of its own. It was not an offshoot of a physical atom.

Evolution has produced myriads upon myriads of different strains of life, most of which failed in the great experiment that was being conducted and became extinct. Most of the remainder of the forms of life became adapted to their environment and thus, having reached their equilibrium, are only living memories of a vanished past. As one great naturalist put it, "The masterpieces of adaption are only the leftovers of evolution." Man has never adapted. Man, therefore, progresses.

Along the uneven course of upward evolutionary progress appeared the mammals, one very small branch of the tree of life. But they had consciousness, and among these mammals suddenly appeared man, who in the course of time had placed within him the power of speech, the ability to contemplate. He developed self-consciousness and conscience along with his abstract thinking. He is unlike all others in life in these respects. He alone can look inward on himself and backward through time on himself and understand his place in evolution.

It's not the body of man that has been developing but rather the mind. The body of man today is not much better, if any, than that of his early ancestors. But the mind of man has ascended with a rush which is being accelerated and which promises tremendous capacities for the future. From instinct to consciousness to thought to contemplation and from there on to the arts and sciences and the other humanities has been a terrific surge. It seems only well on its way.

Man, given the power to deliberate along with the liberty to choose between good and bad and to shape his own destiny, turned naturally toward spiritual considerations, and when he did, human dignity arrived.

I believe that a careful study of the mind of man leads surely to the idea of the supreme mind, the supreme of spirituality, to what we call God. It seems almost inevitable to accept the idea of a transcendent extra-earthly force to explain life represented by the mind of man.

Man considered as a particle of living matter only slightly different from other animals blots out the moral side of man and negates any meaning for individual life.

It is difficult to know when evidence reached the point of proof, particularly when dealing with nonphysical concepts.

Would it not be a tremendous step forward for man if he did not have to depend mostly on belief with respect to immortality? Science has explored all the material elements, the composition of stars, the violence of the atom, and many diseases of the body. Science is carefully studying the brain and knows how damage or abnormality can affect the workings of the mind. But science has, during most of these years of study, by-passed the mind itself. It has left almost untouched the central question of life. To understand the intangible represented by mind is worthy of the efforts of the greatest of our scientists.

There have been some efforts made along these lines in recent decades. Hypnosis and psychiatry are examples. Psychosomatic medicine, recognizing as it does that the mind, and not germs or bacteria, causes many of our bodily ailments, seems to be coming into its own. Also parapsychology, looked upon until recently as almost a superstition, is being recognized today by important universities through the establishment of departments.

A friend of mine, Dr. J. B. Rhine, has such a department at Duke University. Studies are being made there and elsewhere of mental manifestations.

I wish there were more schools of higher education working in this field. It has been proven—at least it has been proven to my satisfaction—that the mind of any particular individual has capacities that reach beyond the body. I refer to telepathy, awareness of things going on at a distance, the ability to move objects beyond physical touch.

The indications are plentiful that mind can transcend time and space and perhaps look even into the future. These extrasensory perceptions seem to be the standard equipment of individual personality, although not evenly distributed, perhaps because of their newness in the evolution of man. Does not all this indicate that mind, if capable of action independent to some degree of the space and time system of nature, is essentially immortal? If there is a part of consciousness that is capable of intercommunication, is it not reasonable to assume that such capability is also in process of evolution from generation to generation and that it can in time reach the sublime, or may I say the divine?

We can chart our physical ancestry at least for a few generations back. I wonder, however, if we know who our mental ancestors were. The mind may not be that bodybound. There may be a pool of mind power, of spiritual force, which gives the body and its console, the physical brain, fleeting existence as an organized unit.

The scientists who have studied this nonphysical side of man have given me belief in the essentials held to by my parents; that is, in the divineness of things and in immortality of the mind.

Karl Menninger, outstanding psychiatrist, in his book *The Human Mind,* has a theoretical talk with a member of the Gospel in which Menninger says, "You may retain steadfastly your faith that there is something divine about the human being and that his faith in God is an essential part of him."

An outstanding nuclear physicist, Dr. William G. Pollard, executive head of the Oak Ridge Institute of Nuclear Research, is also a priest of the Episcopal Church. He explains scientifically the cosmic drama which started the universe on its way and also the slow evolution of man from small cell to what man now is; and after referring to the state of the universe when it was everywhere lifeless, inert and wholly unaware of its own existence, he adds, "But still there was hidden in it even then the potential to generate within itself in the far-distant future a creature . . . to apprehend the far-flung glory of creation . . . and to respond in awed wonder to the majesty of the Holy Author of it all."

The late Dr. LeComte du Nouy was a widely recognized scientist in the fields of biophysics and biochemistry, an associate member of the Rockefeller Institute and the head of a division of the Pasteur Institute. In the late forties he wrote a book called *Human Destiny*. He stated that the purpose of the book was to examine critically the scientific data accumulated by man and to derive therefrom logical and rational consequences. He added, and I quote, "We shall see that these consequences lead inevitably to the idea of God."

He also added that "The destiny of man is not limited to his existence on earth. . . . He exists less by the actions performed during his life than by the wake he leaves behind him, like a shooting star. . . . This is a kind of impersonal immortality of which we are sure. True, individual immortality escapes rational conception, but is hardly questionable if we admit the reality of the wake."

And then there was the Jesuit priest, the late Father Pierre Teilhard de Chardin, outstanding biologist and paleontologist, whose many and outstandingly recognized scientific works dealing with the wonder of man reconciled such evolution with Christian theology and strengthened his belief in the Christian faith and in immortality of soul or mind.

Finally, in the current June issue of *Reader's Digest*, I saw a statement by Dr. Wernher von Braun, who is well known in the fields of missiles and rocketry. He said, "Anything science has taught me—and continues to teach me—strengthens my belief in the continuity of our spiritual existence after death."

These scientists and others like them carry weight with me.

After a half century without reading the Bible, I turned once more to the first chapters of Genesis. The rib, the whale and the ark were still fable, folklore and fancy to me. It is evident that the author recorded from his own limited points of reference, that he was probably a keeper of the flocks and certainly was neither a geologist nor a physicist nor an astronomer. But he also had vision and intuition when he stated that God formed man of material substances but breathed into him the breath of life and thereby man became a living soul. Knowledge and everlasting life were also made available to that man.

Religion, just like man, has been in process of evolution. In the process, religion has taken many forms and adopted many rites. There are theologians who have traced the origins of Christianity back through multiple gods and sun worship, even back to fetishism. These steps in progress are just as natural in spiritual evolution as instinct is in the development of conscious and spiritual man. The Twenty-third Psalm is no less great because limited by these reference points and couched in terms of sheep, pasture, shepherd and still waters.

It's not difficult to be religious if one deals with essentials and if the idea is to reach the summit of faith and understanding without too much detailed inner debate as to which of the many available paths upward is to be chosen.

The Epistle of St. James in Verse 27 of Chapter 1 defines religion at the time the Christian religion was born, in the following language:

"Pure religion and undefiled before God and the Father is this: to visit the fatherless and widows in their affliction and to keep himself unspotted from the world."

A great Christian writer expressed belief in God as follows: "To believe in God is to desire His existence and what is more, to act as though He existed."

Members of the Class of 1960, I leave you with that thought and one further observation:

A part of you that you meet up with every minute in the day is animal governed greatly by instincts that were imbedded in your brain over the many hundreds of thousands of years while your spiritual side was in the very early stages of evolving. Some of these instincts are still needed. But most of them come down from the time when, without knowledge of good or bad, it was kill or be killed. These particular instincts are no longer needed. The non-needed ones will in time get weak to the point of disappearance. Until that time man, with liberty of action, must choose between these still strong but dying instincts of the animal self or the new and growing inner spiritual self.

I hope you will all choose wisely.